Trpypanda

Trpypanda

Contraband

Jean Jabril Joseph

ISBN: 0692848851
ISBN 13: 9780692848852

Content

Acknowledgments

Thank you, all of you beautiful souls for helping mend together this vibration of a gift into the world.

Clarity

The past, present, and moments; the symbiosis of our lives—our births, our lives, our deaths—all tied into a single package that we spend our time on this earth unwrapping.

Sometimes we clearly see what we are staring at, but sometimes we do not. Sometimes things happen to distract or deceive us, and we must take more careful notice of what we hold dearest, or we risk the chance of losing ourselves.

11/07/Undefined

We are living art expressing poetry. Thus the ransom to our happiness is all around us—if only you could see it! If only they could understand it! Within all creation, within all the universe, we became aware that we were in what we seek—a sleep doorway away, art expressing art, the undeniable truth of eternity's birth.

Poetry Reporter

Bring onto you, the here-and-now descriptive understandings: repolish, remodel. Your perspective views, my perspective understandings watch from afar. Relentless, conjuring, remolding, reshaping, regurgitating your moments. Press to print; where's the press?

This is the view of sight, re-conjure it into a gift, shape it into an art form, spread it out to the world.

Let you absorb the fragments of my understanding. Let it become your perception, our perception! So art survives…

We pour things in alternative terms—a paradigm combined with a conundrum, stitched and mended with a paradox. Tell me what your pair of eyes can see. If you are in the pits of darkness, I will uplift you from the pits of night and uphold you in the day of love, along with the day of art. Our perception is one of heart.

These poetries I report to you are the stories of the world's view. They are love, and the world is you.

Paradox

The answer lies within the shifting paradigms of your perception. Thus creating a canvas of what you deem to be reality!

Aura

I'm intoxicated in my aura; you can see me sense me from a mile away, arriving while wide awake!

Do be humble, less frightful, for I am not in the company of pain nor sorrow, yet for your keepsake, I'll set free the shackle chains and shower you with roses of life and death, discussing mortality.

Take a seat, for the affections have already taken their path, and I have deprived you of your thoughts, stumbling and having you under less than your present self.

It's hard to breathe; I'm levitating.

Attach your wavering heart to my compression of your crumbling dreams. The shatters are loud, but my warmth muffles out and eradicate our waves of hatred.

My smiles change shapes, forming your emotional I believe under the intoxication of my aura-elixir. We are reborn into our endless world!

Fruitful

I looked into my world from a glass cup, beautiful as snow! A tree grows into the blue, extended beyond infinity.

Submerge into our abilities of water-soul; my world was upside down, but I savored the taste that remained printed against the wrinkled crevice of my mouth; I let it linger as it rolled down my tongue, swishing back and forth against my cheek like inner tides.

I severed the bonds; she looked at me with a cigarette in her mouth, clenching her beautiful brown skin. Silk!

Teasing me with the curve of her breast, she stares into me, and I yearn for her.

My ideals are fruitful; they lay seeds while the world takes a bite, and I take a seat with a faithful bow.

Mother Nature

My smile petals, my rose that has the ends of my love petals. There's an end to no road that I walk. Each path is divinely beautiful because of my magical paint brush. Yes! My rose, my petal, you are my brush. You paint me the image of my eternal love. I love you, the one.

I need the color of light brown. Pay close attention; I will grow it closest to the ground. Here's a circle that looks like eyes penetrating deep into mines. Yes, yes! Okay, I need the color of darkest night, a black rose. Yes, yes. Black rose. The strings, the streaks, the silky—you remind me of the wonderful soothing hair of the breeze. Yes! I will need the color of ancient Africa. Yes, the color—the silky, brown-skin, chocolate coating—that's great for the filling. I need it, I need it. It's my skin, magnificent brown petal.

I'm barely able to breathe now! Give me…give me my color. Give me the color of the lips; give me my pink rose…rose beautiful blossom petal…pink rose…

Give me…give me my petals of sky blue. The sky! I'm not feeling quite blue. Give me…give me my petal white. Yes, I will draw you clouds. Everything must be just right. You are the most beautiful thing I've ever created. You are my nature; beautifully wild you are. You're my wife; yes, you're my rose petal. I love you.

Detach

To be slow is to be detached. To be detached is to be free of the egotistical mind and the illusions it contains!

Bare Me

Haste in my walk, pace in my presence, urgency in my run—my takeoff is abrupt.

My hair is wild, like wool floating ragefully in the wind.

My fascination is griping, appalling, and awing. I urge you to bare me, hold me, and carry me, for I am the one who helps create your world, your reality.

To hold tightly is to worry no more, as long as this "here and now is captured," the strings of this harp will scream songs of your beating heart that cast a melody of hope. I was born for this purpose.

Eternal Dreams
External World

The flow moves with every wave and ripple of life. My heart beats as a stone; therefore, time stops and sleeps alone.

When spirits and souls alike gain their wings, the universe becomes their world. Great wings of joy and happiness spread through the vines of life.

Yet we dream of the world of our inner self where life is our own, our eyes never waken, and we dream of a blind man's song—deaf, deaf, deaf from your mind, your body!

Sleep deafly to the cry of your soul, your inner strength lost in a dream world. Break, break out as hard as you can, but tumble into the endless stream of dreams.

Get out! Get out! A scream of wisdom so loud, so ancient, so old that it breaks the fabric of the world. Dreams to each his / her own are no longer our homes.

Breathe

My bong has the universe in it, and I know because I inhale it. So when I speak, please understand that our universe is what we breathe, and when we exhale, we live beyond heaven or hell!

Bed

You lie on me; you're comfortable every evening. You make my nerves jump. Calm down spring. You lie with me through the seasons, but you do it the most on the weekends.

Good evening. How have you been? You've been away too…what felt like a century. Breaking into a new world, you love me. You gave me your attention. What's wrong this evening? You tell me nothing. Where are you? What is that burning aroma? It's tragedy! Why am I going up in flames? Why can't I budge? Why can't I escape? Is it because my size, or for the simple fact that I'm a queen? No! I'm your bed. I'm no more because I was yours.

Embrace

D ays pass. I am not what I once was. I rock back and forth in front of my porch! These are my days, the days when my body no longer wanders; in its place, my mind takes flight to travel far and wide. My porch, my porch is the departure spot, where my mind takes off and forgets all the corpse it left behind. With these moments I have come to see more worlds within worlds. Objects and beast alike have mastered the element of flight; they are swift as warheads and strike as comics from the cosmos. Telepathic minds oversee the vast body of the universe, where pathways are no longer made out of trees of life, but the thirst of man changes enough to quench the string of eternity. I have traveled many eons and have seen many moons; nonetheless, I am missing two youth. Only once retained can I strip free of the bonds that restrain me. This is a thought that my famished mind fails to grasp in its entirety. No! No! No! I'm being drawn back, drawn back like an animal losing its grip on its prey. No!!! Without body and time, I am not able to feast on the unknown. Home again to my porch, my porch, the chain to this world. Back and forth I went; in front of my swing of a porch. It came back to you, we left time notes I will always reach you!

Whisper

Swing on city's lights, over bright daylight! I'm not afraid of heights; I'm free as a bird. I like the fashion in which the kite takes the clouds in its glide, twirling upwardly with a majestic stride.

The scenery is smoky gray and swirly milky white! I like the structure of the buildings; I feel free as a kid as the wind blows through my hair and whispers in tongues of ancient tales I've never heard.

My tired sheet is beneath me. The chain holds my place—a safety net if I would ever leave the nest, but I'm not quite found of roller coasters! But this here is a trip in a road, in a path, that I would gladly fall over on.

I like parasailing. Let me free dive, land on a ship, and sail to the end of the earth—only to repeat the cycle while knowing that I lived life. Yet my humble beginning was forged in the moment of love as I was taken to the air by a push! Back and forth I went until I took flight to these brave new worlds of multiple realities, as I left it all behind.

Enlightenment

Hi! I will sexually intrigue your mind, tenderly caress your thoughts until you're mine. Wonders of influence, mind boggling, mind draining—ecstasy! A high of enlightenment! Integrity, I will bring forth out of you. Naked before me.

Baffle me into senselessness, wordless. Make every bit of it worth it. Only then will I have your body—more of the same, better than anybody. Yes, you should be ashamed, but I'll rap you up as a gift and put a bow on you! You're my gift. Christmas has not arrived, but you're my own holiday, so run to it. You're my mate.

Owl

I have been given a rooster voice. So tell me why would the night owl raise the sun? For if he does, his world will be no more. Why would the night owl with his rooster voice raise the sun to its center peak? For if he does, his world will be no more.

The owl with its rooster voice begins to sing, and with each note he makes, his world begins to fade. And inch by inch, he begins to feel the warmth of the sun and this feeling he never felt before. So with a deep breath, he sings, and with each note, the sun rises until it reaches its center peak.

The owl with the rooster voice has noticed something: the warmth of the sun is gone and along with it his world! In its place is brightness, an inferno so enraged that it scorches his very core.

Now he yearns for his world, before the light, before the pain, and with an eclipse, his world returns to him, and although it was not long, he yearns for his home.

"The owl with the rooster voice."
The voice of the rooster was hope, and the sun was love.
The owl was you.

You Should Know

No! My kiss was the physical symbolism of the manifestation of the repro-ductive desire of fluctuation we call love.

Familiar

A. A. A. Who, you? Yes, you! You look familiar. Your smile, your eyes—the windows of you, your soul.

Your eyes, they're so familiar. Hi, have we met?

You look…I feel like it's something like déjà vu, like you're my friend, like we're no longer foes but something like kin.

Are you my sister? Are you my brother? Are you me? Yes. Hi! Hold my hands. Can you tell me my future? No? Yes? Help me breathe; hold my hands. Guide me above. Can we be one? Yes, but we stand still. Can we move? Can we run?

No! Let's take flight. These are our wings. The sky's our home. Yes, yes, dust! Rain of the sun!

View

Your perception of days doesn't get longer, yet your illusions that you create extend as far as the world around you.

My Woman

My woman, my woman should be unique as my style, cute as my smile. Yes! My woman, my darlin', my lady, my baby, the mother of my child. The way she walks, the way she talks attracts all.

She's one of a kind! Make each and every one of you wonder. She's a perfect picture of a model—yes! Your daughter, her beauty is divine. Her grace cannot be defined. She's not of this world. She's a doll—a perfect image of you all!

Infinitely

C arry on in between a hasty road of two arms, skateboard performing simi-larly as a ballerina, and yes the technique was perfected with elegance. I'm a rebel! I fall in the air; I stunt hard, but I land in my ballerina grace with style and tender care.

I execute a one-sixty suspended in midair, in midflight. I pose for both! I got my Chucks on and my ballerina ribbons to go along. Who says that I can't have my cake and eat it too?

Ballerina skate shoes, we rule! And yet I yelled and advised the officer that I'm five years old.

I see the marking of a label on your vehicle: P.O.L.I.C.E. Police, I see…

Please help me; my older, seven-year-old brother is holding a revolver, and I don't think it's going to be a tomorrow. Believe me: I'm not afraid, but I love.

Allow me to freeze this moment and jump into suspended animation in my black gown. Frozen in gray, the clouds grant me freedom.

The sand below my feet marks my path, an imprint resembling birth, a heart.

This embryo within me will receive an abundance of love, so when the moment arrives, we can secure unfathomable bonds and stare into the reflection of what we once were physically and yet are infinitely!

Egyptian

You and I can get high and lie side by side and fly like angels in the sky and just watch the world die. Hear the ancient Egyptians cry with all their might, "We're united in this eternal night."

Wayne

Forgetful-minded, are you lost in the trenches of today, overdo the moment, over succeeding, triumphing and trampling and Goliath stance, rise as a king sit as a god.

Misconstrued, misconceived—firing off on all cylinders, laying species of seeds. They grow bright. What is in my mind is lowering dim lights, synapses sparking off and inaccurately putting me to sleep. Codeine! Prescription indeed. I pray on my knees, amen! Lord, please…

I play the game that wins me. This rap game wraps me in the blanket of confidence, wraps me with humanity's blessings.

Take a notepad and misdocument me; take a mic and misrepresent me, stabbing and mutilating me like the late Caesar—with hope of death coming out your instruments of greed. I'm the critical disease.

But the world knows that I'm here—a caution that I take. Slow me down to brake. I slumber; then I awake.

Tomorrow is not mine, but I reach for the here and now, building gold-mines out of my mind. Seizure, Pimp-C, can you see, see these things in my sleep? Don't count me out; I'm still in, counting the days to my end.

I have my camp here, and we're winning. Wayne is a historical figure for your age and momentum. Keep this genre, for this is a favor. Life is a gift, and these TMZ reporters are piranhas with fevers.

Passenger

Who said being in the passenger seat was ever normal? It's as difficult as being the driver. Safety first! I jumped out the window—free field, free fall—in hopes that I'd drown in the world, in my own pool of hopes and dreams. I grew again like weed from the soil. I peel and I pluck and I blow. Who knew your food smelled like the wind blowing good? Open the window and enjoy the sunshine.

I stared at it and lost the gaze. I soared like all life, looked down and seen I had no legs, but I pondered about it and just lingered and just landed, asking for a lending hand, because I will need one just for tomorrow, if it ever comes. For I have been waiting for a very long time, and I haven't found a purpose, but if I sit down and drew an image of it…

It would be a screw so that I can nail down my hopes, my dreams, my essence in order for it to be spread throughout the galaxy. But you have to understand me; you have to see me. I'm looking for a gal who can see me. Silly me, it was never true, but they all walk up to me, and I walk into them.

For one day, take my place and walk in my path, for when they take my eyes and view my world…For one second, claim my heart along with all the emotions that are attached to it. String my hope and joy, and let them beat through your veins and let them become your lifeline because I loved you. Mother, I loved you; ancestors, I've always spoke the truth.

Spoken

If I've ever spoken to an angel, then I did yesterday. You have the smile of a Nubian queen, thighs and eyes of a goddess, and lips of rose petals. You are of heavenly descent—my dream!

The Beach

The smell of it when I pass by causes me to reminisce. The breeze mixes with it, taking me to a place that I muse over. I really miss the way she cast her sight full glare on me.

I walk into her; she engulfs me, draws me in, and pushes me out. Sometimes she gets frantic, and I drown in her midst, reemerging stronger and purer than before.

She's been around well over the creations of calculated moments, before the sun's birth and the stars' rise. In the blanket of night, I dive deep into her. She dives above me. I died in her!

She rebirths me; she provides me nourishment, refreshes me and rejuvenates me!

I run with her. He sees me; he's afraid of me. I want to pull him in, but I'm too vast! I'm a titan, a goliath compared to him! I want to cradle him. I'm afraid I might hurt him. Well I'll become his flare of a sun; he'll be my moon. I'll love and gaze onto him from a distance.

Humanity has called me the waterfront, yet I am more than that! Beseech and behead—I will stand forth to only behold something that I can't ever grasp, slipping away because I have neither structure nor stability. I can't maintain; I am too free for him to ever conceive.

I was never the waterfront, more the ocean—a nickname that never molded me.

Lake of Stars

Side by side, lakes of stars, skies of lakes reflect heaven's gate. Perfect scenery, perfect image—you can call it my centerpiece. Moments cannot be spoken but understood—a work of art that can't be remembered, but is immortalized.

Waves of dreams. Emotion screams! Loudly, breathe slowly, exhale tenderly. Touching one another's lips trembling. Kindred spirits, you and I. A match in heaven's eyes!

Morning Haze

The moment you and I stood by and let the flow of ours run dry—don't consider it to be a misconception of love or a misunderstanding of what could have been, because what could have been would be, and what was has been! So don't create a false illusion of yesterday, and don't try to create tomorrow, for tomorrow and yesterday I'm afraid are one and the same.

Let me dwell on now, and allow me to love you for now, for the creation of thought I conjured will become my vision. So let me be careful of my steps, and let us whine and dine until we arrive with me having tea with you in the morning haze; you had tea with me through life.

It's you and me on this meadow of a physical plain to only continue to play around. I promise we will never fall, for the object that was given the title "plain" was never created. We had wings. The way you speak to me is the way I perceive the concept of a butterfly flying through summer. You make me warm inside. You, you, and you!

Understand that it was not when you spoke but the moment you arrived that piqued my interest, so don't create the illusion that I'm not here, that I don't exist or that you don't, because we are. That illusion is a blindfold that keeps you from understanding truth.

Hatred and dislike are only born the moment you create them—transforming themselves into disabilities. Relinquish them and you will obtain stability.

Equality is the gift we give to one another, together for eternity. Humanity is to bear no shame in it, for this world is an orchestra of symphonies, and we move both up and down like the flow of a river or the stream of a wave.

Our emotions are who we are, so let us let go of the blindfold of our own creation, of our own doing. I love you more than you will know, so I'd rather just tell you than show you forever more.

Create

D on't trust me; believe in me! Most souls don't have the will to create; I'm creating at this very moment.

Fly Hello

I sit in a seat that draws me in. I sit in a seat the pulls me very deep within, to fall into an endless depth, where I feel detached from my very flesh. Tears fall from my eyes, and memories begin to fade. I cannot speak, cannot hear sound. Different shades of gray my hair begins to fade—wisdom peeling off—while the 'why of moments' continues fluently changing shape and form.

I came into energy; I came into the meaning of existing, into the continuum of forever.

You tell me! What of it I cannot see? In return I shall tell you what the world knows, and you will tell me of their understanding.

I will disappear before you come, before you reach a century of life within the tides of God! Of all of creation! But we of humanity write literature books of lies and engrave them with different titles of disguise. Yet I will not cry, for the world shed tears for you, tear drips of rain drops far from our skies. For everything that was once hidden you called hide! What a simple veil. I bid you farewell!

For Sure

You have me, but I own you! I vow your stream will flow, but promise me not to scream as you climax out of your mind and into our soul.

Wave

Dive into the clouds' high mountain peaks. I seek a path of release! Jagged clouds, jagged cliffs, jagged rocks—can you see the jagged features in my smile? Take off clothing, bare to the skin like glove, like a suit! Buy you a suit, bio suit! A container—so how would it feel to be another container? Join another contain only to be one container. It waves, and I wave eternally back; it waved and I waved eternally back! As I felt myself being pulled towards it, I was in the air, the gentle winds caressing, the breeze soothing me. I breathed when it took me to the waves—the sound crashing against my body, my vessel ripping me into shreds of memories. I was released into the wave of your good by parties. You were early whenever I began.

Appetite Galore

Thank you for having the preconceived notion that I am a lamb without the ability to part ways from the heard.

Nonetheless I will eat your heart and rip out your ambitions from your throat with a simple gesture of my smile.

Your pleas will trickle down onto my ears and touch the soil of a long-gone paradigm. Farewell my friend. Swell, sweet entrance—into hell you go!

Reflection of Reflection

Standing tall as a branch while ages fall through my hands and linger in skin as I crack like glass of time…

Hair flows against my back like cold serenity waterfalls resembling the moments of my life.

Tears sketch the world below my heart and above my hopes. Vulture seeking for the moment I fall. I cry!

The stumbles that I take…You can see the anguish and the pain in my face. The wrinkles they create resemble cracks through the chattered window of my soul (meadow), but I stand tall, beautiful, and lean.

I strive as it fixes its gaze upon the demonic creatures I created. My pet, my pain will reflect through the rain; my cracks, my imperfections will become my gifts. And for this I stand immortal, a perfect memorial, a memento to your memories.

Deep

I crave a love so deep that the ocean would be insecurely jealous, and the end of time would become our home. I crave a love so vast that we become the meaning of space itself! So close your eyes and have me...

Anniversary

At this moment we met, and in return, I recited the feelings we felt. You corrected me, and we became greater. I atoned for your sins, and I became stronger while we together obtained all the flavors of wisdom.

We undrape each other to discover that the dreams and needs of one another were created in this moment. That moment, that anniversary was created in our images, and with our love we crafted and constructed the wings that all creation had bestowed upon us.

Thus allowing this love, our love, to continually and forever soar endlessly, surpassing heaven and earth and creating a new realm where you and I became life. This anniversary marks our beautiful story, my love, so let's let this moment continue on its journey. I love you!

Immediately

I love eating her oyster, while she leaves her pearl on my tongue! Infatuated. She's moist; I swallow her twice. My lips are dripping wet. She moans as I cradle her clam up to my tongue and devour the ocean out of her.

Inside

About me! I'm a king and so are you. A queen that can move boundaries, and so are you! I am both balance, I am both into you, and you are separate. About me! I am a symbol of all of you. About me? I'm loyal like your prayers, joyful like your Saturday mornings when you were a child!

Playful when you and I, we, were in the playground enjoying the hide-and-go-seek of our grade school. Never did we imagine about me that I would come to view the world in its form—a marvelous creature with us being souls inside of creatures!

I'm sorry if I'm losing you, but remember it's about me—yet in the same instance a symbol of you! Allow me to capture you and let you see that you're truly free to express what you please.

So I repeat it every moment without any type of compliments or gratification. No applause because I'm proud of you!

The shimmer of my reflection seems to ripple back at us from the rivers of my forefathers, transforming us and giving rise to a bridge that awaken me. About me. I'm carefree, but I'm captivated like the wings of a bird. I'm intoxicated by no boundaries.

I am courage, I am strength, I am joy, I am the gratification, and I am the moment within the here and now! I was; I am you, about me! I am all of you as you are me. Please ignore my physical, for we are beyond words.

Purple Kush

Your purple grape and apple leaves are intrinsic. Your grape and apple leaves are remarkably beautiful and gazed at and trapped in ways that elude my mind's capabilities. Enchanted, endowed with such a grace—your grape apple leaves leads up to hairs of snow, glazing through your richness. It's the orgasm of glister from my love, creating a web of mystical frost.

Drape you with orange tentacles and let you soothe me as I taste you, pluck you, grind you, and lay you out so gently to your bed. Rolled, you tuck, kiss your good-nights and light your dreams—infected, flooded, and gas it with chain breaking, illusion stripping.

The silencer to my physical mind were set free…ugh. I love your apple, green, white frost, orange tentacles…I love you! You, my grape, apple, white as frost hairs with orange tentacles, I love you Purple Kush… I love you!

Reflection

When encountering your reflection and deem yourself to be your own worst enemy, take heed that you have set the tone for your destiny.

Greatness Drawn

Mighty, stern, stubborn gaze upon my frightfulness. Lose sense of yourself. Hypnotic, hypnosis, under my trance I command, but with humble grace, I yawn as a king.

You yearn for the leadership that radiates off this union of us! Let days roll onto water ripples of my stride; I am the mirage of royalty.

I stare onto you, inside of you, only to awaken the greatness inside of you.

I walked inside our booth while anxiety clinched its grip onto me. The receiver picked up my trembling hand, and I was engulfed and I became submerged in mirror waters!

Submerge under pressure instantly. Sea life swimming beneath me, in front of me, behind me—such intense pressure is what you created in me.

I must always cry out the truth, for the pressure would've drowned me.

Cry

It seems though every time the heavens cry, the earth begins to feast and come alive.

Bridge Grave

I'm under a bridge. I'm attached; it is attached. The way it designs me, the way it captures me…I'm youthful, for which you see forever, beautiful and tamed, intact. Bystanders' stare at me—beautifully divine, the vines rap around me and the branches reach out to you.

They caress your skin, the structure of my image. Roses bloom from my lengthy hair—green leaves the strains! A bouquet is given, but nothing can be enough for the damsel's beautiful grave.

Despise You

We have the uncanny ability to reincarnate within all individuals the reason why they completely despise our existence, outside the conscious awareness of our current existence.

Legacy

You are my legacy. I will provide you with all my secrets so that you can provide to your young, for it will be reborn and recaptured in a new image.

You will be able to orchestrate these secrets of lessons how you see fit. I give my all to you, and in return I live through you. Thus the course of pattern continues. You relive in your children throughout the generations to come—after you, after them, and you after me!

The Exit

While I disappear beneath the waters' depths, I throw my hands above the surface, signing, "Fuck the rest!"

Live Life

It was like a moment that I couldn't recall, a feeling I couldn't remember, a touch I couldn't distinguish—all of it seems familiar! All of it felt like home; all of it felt like a place I'd been. In the universe's sleepless dreams, in places and endless streams I couldn't reach, but today at this second, I felt it all…

I was completely given to it; I wanted it to continue. It caressed me in such a way that levitation took my place. I kissed it, and it kissed me, I loved it! It cherished me.

How we are, how you are…the life that sustains me? The moment I perceived it, I could never, ever, ever let it go. The understanding that you taught me, that it's impossible, even in the moment and in the act of me releasing you!

It's the same sequence of moment in which I gained you. Pour me into your life, and let me soothe you. Let me drink you, so that I quench for more. I took you, and worn, you fell to the floor, and I tore myself into you. We fitted each other! I embraced you, and at that moment, we arrived, we arrived to what we call life live.

Swing

It was captured in midair. It took me and froze me. I reminisce; I took the backstreet, picked up the frame and stared into it.

The moment was relit, rekindled. The flame of joy that coursed through me was alive again.

All those steps, the snow white sky, the green-like clouds I drew on the playground floor…I knew then that it would be warm, that I would walk these lands.

I swung her front and back. She held me in enjoyment. I felt her heart beat with excitement. Her grip clinched even tighter.

The joy phased as he let go…

It was remarkable! He landed without any type of hesitation. The moment was there; my home was over. The tree grows makers of moments. This was a remarkable moment marked with the signatures of never-ending.

Robotic Heart

Here's a rose for my love, my friend. I'm cold as steel; I have robotic eyes, yet I can sense the feelings that flow between you and me!

Let the shadow of my affection grace your smile and greet your emotions.

Let the shadow of my lesser self caress your blinded notion so that one day you can defrost my frosted heart.

Wouldn't Know

I don't know. Sometimes I think you want me to show more affection. It's not that! It's just hard for me to believe! If I was to do the things you have done to me, you would feel the same. If you were to lose the things I have lost, you would feel the same, but then again I don't know how you would feel.

Rewind

Uncontrollably the moment stands. Enter her gaze. I'm lost for words; I'm lost for days! She spoke words the caused trimmers and trembles to echo throughout my soul. Made my physical, made my moth-dry like the Sierra...

I cough dust. My heart mummifies.

I prayed to my mother and seen her grave—testimonial, my testimony! She confessed more than words, months, and days ahead; it was a glimpse of reality that shook the vibration within me. It was that simple! I took the marrow from her and drenched myself with its reflections of me!

I took the answers and inscribed them onto all the broken pieces of broken emotions. Similarities took place, but my raw action engulfed me under the roar of its own conviction: the reflection of my self-worth.

It erased everything and brought me back to the beginning. You can add each moment...And at the end of it all, I couldn't disappear! I remained visible, tolerant, and firm. She looked at me as her tongue and lips uttered, "My heart beats for another."

Tears ran down my cheeks. It was within that moment her reality revealed itself to me, disturbing my space of blissfulness and shaking the fabric of my essence.

I and she were two different souls! What I'd burdened, what I'd carried was different from what she had borne! I carried the space of the galactic universe while she carried a feather!

Yet it was enough for her to change direction. She looked at me and asked me how? And smiled. I smiled in return and told her that my secret is my love! My love is what gave me the strength to carry the space in which all galaxies reside. I'm sorry I couldn't return it to you; I'm sorry you couldn't see it in time—may be in the next lifetime. I'm just a phone call away!

With Me

You weren't of any absence in order for me to transfer my thoughts onto a physical item to be given to you. For you were with me during my creation of confessions to you.

Grace

In a world of my own, I create a haze of multiple lives. I paint with my journey's joy and agonies. I am proud, for you have uplifted me along with your grace, sheltering my dreams. I praise you as you anoint my lips, my hands, my cheeks, and my heart.

I uplifted the texture of my features and let the stride of my hair grace the end of my back while my smile encored to your everlasting love. I have no worries; I can travel for miles.

I close my eyes, and I pray to you gifts of gratitude as mercy befalls me. I thank you, truthfully! For my days are with you until the rest of my life has flown home to you!

Truth of Trust

S eek it, and it will find you. Embrace it, and it will set you free! For you are who you have always been.

She not a pub, nor a pilsner

I know she's exotic I know she got imported, but you know I can't have her without the chaser. it's imperative that I mix her! When I poured her into my inner space; she took the shape of my ego

She had me mentally confined, her champagne French body had me at complete attention as I sipped her entire body slowly! I have to chase her, because she needs me.

I want to sip every bit of her. I could feel her elixir twisting my tongue in directions I would've never performed alone. I want to quench my lust only with her!

The way she wets my lips and wets my tongue maliciously miraculously; leaves me with a marinating shivering in my mouth. With an aftertaste that I cannot begin to describe, the way she let me get high off of her allows me to lose myself in her.

I mean she slowly severed my worries, my concerns she erased them all, my pains she subdued them, the broken fragments of my heart; she mends them! I loved her.

I loved the way she made me feel inside, the way she made me perceive the things around me, allowed me to witness life's transformation without worries.

for at that moment of bliss I crystalized her into a gift, but don't try to give her to me and don't try to overdose me with her because I can't handle all of her!

I'm afraid she would over power me at my weakened state. I need her to train me; I just need a portion of her, just a little bit of her. Remember we need her; we need to swallow her!

I wouldn't be the soul I am today without her she supported me. Got my anger under control, but truth be told! It would be times where she would help get that anger out of control, those were the best moments. She's my illusion to our hallucination I need that chaser darling!

Existence

Why live a miserable existence? In this physical life, you can remain a sheep and follow the herd, or you can become the soulful beast you are and devour the oppressors,

Simply become aware of the mind's egoistic regurgitation of collective past experiences. Be attentive to thoughts that one mind continuously has revolving, from the past onto the present. This creates a formulated possibility of what humanity calls the future.

(A figment of one's imagination created by fragmented of past experiences gathered by the mind.)

Wall Street

1973, my intentions were true. Young man, I'm jazzed up; I'm ready! I'm blazed up. Do you see my coat? It's gray, tailor-suited. I'm ready for that financial gain. I got dreams; I got a mission to accomplish. Wall Street titans, I'm about to climb every one of them, every inch of those leviathans. I want to learn!

Dinner table: I'm being coached by the founder. 1. Coke, 2. Heartless, and 3. Barrel deep into their pockets—hot pockets! Spilling money into your pockets—eat their money! You can do far more with it than they can do in their wildest fantasies. I rode that bull until I crashed the course, and I made billions and fucked millions…over!

Bring out the strippers, bring out the guitar, bring out the bankers, bring out the instruments, and bring out the entertainments. I got millions and trillions. I have accomplished. I have deprived and bribed and feasted on their pride while obtaining more riches then I know what to do with. I mean, it's coming out of my jesters, even my mink coat sweaters.

I like that pressure. Every Kama Sutra position, I breathe better. Cocaine—sniff, sniff. I'm sorry. Copacabana, I had it better, got me feeling like Bruce

Banner. HULK!!! Every time I inhaled that snow, it was cocaine flakes, and boy do I love it cold.

Breeze every day, along with my coffee. Running freight trains with my subordinates. She was exhausted on that oak wood desk, and yes it was awkward with that dress. We all received head treatments. The results came in, and we were named, Wolf Pack, Degenerates, Wall Street's pets.

I didn't lie, but to the ninety-nine percent. We ate, we feasted! Until they inflated and blew out. My apologies, we still didn't sink! Hands out, we borrowed and bailed out, remarried—dancing in this ballroom with all my goonies and goons, trumpeting to my joy. I was summoned, but worry not, for I have lived through the fifties and sixties and have tasted my fair share. Enjoy the day love. Learn how to hate trust, and forgive hate forever trusting.

For the one percent was always lusting. Well, I made it. That elite one percent allowed me to rape the ninety-nine percent, and should I tell you the rest of it over cocaine, breeze, and quaalude-714s? I stole your dreams and pocketed your hopes, and the rest was bullshit.

Elude

I would speed up only to return to repeat the process, while collecting the essence of creation itself, thus making me the viewer of the continuum, which the elite of humanity has renamed as time and space in order to elude the masses into mental confinement.

Twin Halloween

Their eyes are glowing. Holding hands, inseparable. In the hallway, the corridor, the twins smile. They yelled, "Halloween is upon!" and the prowl began. Redeem random, please call murder backward, murder me, ransom me. Spell backward, and you will have back in between.

Twins holding hands, marks on their chest. Yell, yell. The tender touch, the friction the immorality of death. Pass begin delivering to unknown. We came to grasp, and took your very own.

Our jaws are extended. Our fangs are out. Glare onto our in-depth, vast, space-less, vessel.

Let us devour you, let us consume you, let us destroy your humanity so we can have you as a playmate.

Balloon Flight

In the living room, and we sit in the living room. Dinner begins. I stare onto my perfectly rounded out blue purple plate. I ate my peas; now allow my hands to form the deceptive construction of peace.

A smile appeared on the poor attempt—futures of a smirk that I plastered on as a display to my plate.

I looked up and seen the moment on the wall. I look outside and notice freedom in the sky; the purple wings spread and merge with the clouds. I was born with ideals of days; I was born in our moments.

Green, pink, purple, and yellow took flight outside of the sky, fusing with lights of our bright sun. It has attached itself to me and tied itself to me; it bounds with life!

I wanted to fly as the handle of our chair was grabbed by you; I ran with it dragging on its feet, allowing the surface beneath my feet to riddle with deformed scars as I made my way to the exit space.

I put it in front of the stares and gazed inside of me and walked back out again, dragging it to the middle of the walkway. I sat on it and looked up again, but I wasn't there.

I gathered the balloons and attached them to the back sheet. I negotiated skies—blues swirling with green, pink, and yellow as I stood above my chair.

I laid both of my arms, surface spread out. My hair was blown back and forth by the curiosity of the wind blessing. I looked upward and began to fly. I began to soar. I, it, and we were one with the balloons and the clouds.

Arrive

When I depart, I would like to arrive at a place that's fun, crazy, and exciting!

A place I can call "my secret"—a place where I can be a kid again and run wild, a place where I can fall asleep without any care in the world, a place like inside your mind and heart, love!

Reflection

That fateful union, that fateful reunion, that simmer, that reflection—the days went along, and I stared and remembered. All along those words, those thoughts travel far. It reached your heart, creating thumps after thumps, bringing you back to life, to me.

We enjoyed and breathed, swinging back and forth in our life tree! My smile is your smile; my mimics are your mimics. Through hardship and pain, to the ravine, and slow to refine, on the ocean waves, our emotions quiver yet hold onto the flames of possibilities: recoiling, respringing, rerouting, and rerooting.

Tears were the substance of our love, our cares, our likes. The night sky has grown beautifully vast and wide like our own.

Close yourself away from me and I far away from you! But these reflections of mirages, these hallucinations, have chained me, locked me. I can't escape; I can't run away because my shadow is of you, and your essence is in me while mine is in you.

What incredible dreams, what incredible views! Your screams, your moans, your cries, your need, and your nature are all surprises.

Soulful, tender—my yawns are your reasons; your reasons are my needs; my needs are your reasons for living; your reason for living is my reason for breathing! Par to par, hand to hand, let this course. This path leads to our hearts. Can you hear it? It's one single beat. Can you feel it? You and me.

You Are

You're not going to be something, because what you are is more! The world has yet to experience your wonders.

Introduce Me

I introduce myself. Can you introduce yourself? Seduce me! I see you came; I see they came. Walk toward one another. Smiles. The body introduces itself, then seduces itself and subtracts itself.

Introduce yourself! Why would you want to know someone like me? Different objectives, different motives. Follow my story—the script is exciting! Trust…me! I came in two and two, embraced you, studied you, embraced you, studied you, and brick by brick, wall by wall, structure by structure, dream after dream, vision after vision, and clime of serene ships, submit onto' you've claimed my ambition built the shape and the images of my heart, my love, my foundation the moment I laid eyes on you.

Let me introduce me: I am yours; I am your lover, your dreams; I am your moments, and I am your friend; I am your screams, your hatred; I am your joy; I am your solvation, and together we are knitted into the heart of god to be reborn into life again.

Kindred understanding, past every life extension, we will always intertwine. Infinite is our sweet design, and if you would have it, I will be honored to introduce you to you.

Within

If you have potential, then opportunity is an attraction! And when both begin to intertwine, a newfound reality is brought forth.

Awaken Love

The storm came without any warnings. I was naive! I closed my eyes and dreamt. I fell into a fog of despair. My heart was ripped apart, and I was the chaos that was creating it all. Tears fell in a place that formed my face, and they came from the overflow of my emotions, a sadness so in-depth that I couldn't begin to imagine.

I lived a life of death, yet everybody believed I was living. I couldn't conceive what was happening, until I saw that moment! The moment that never came. They told me that moments don't exist! Just call it time, call it days, and call it years…

I lived in agony. My heart was ripped apart, but my love kept me sane. They told me it was insane. It was never the same until the sun burst into my world and made me feel in ways I never felt.

Truth raised me to the highest levels of understanding and set far apart a guilt so in-depth that I could not begin to understand, but when I saw pain engulf my world, I wanted to save hers. I reached out with all my might and gave bearing to myself—at the same time, in the same instant, obtaining her life and mine simultaneously.

We grew wings in worlds of other worlds. The blanket of galaxy that humanity called home, we created! And every day was a smile, and every moment was one of no regrets. These are love. So I tell you, who's been through much, that I know love and that I can say I love you.

Fall in Love

I speak of the pure emotion of being in love itself, which doesn't care about humanity's methods of bonds, thus creating its own profound intertwining complexity of connections.

So you are and will fall in love when you least expect it.

I Speak

Picked up the frame, the portrait, a beautiful image, a masquerade! The vibrant shade of my eyelashes complements the curve of my lips, the length of my hairs and the curls they form, a design of spring curls within curls.

The frame, the portrait of glazed eyes reflects my agony, gracefully enchanted, but the pursuer condemns me, hence putting away my facial allure. I can't breathe; the grips of hands around my neck are suffocating me.

What you see is not the polarity of my shattered glare of a reflection but a loop of scattered shards resembling our inner demise.

Blanket Universe

In the cosmos stars, I sleep united with the beginning of creation, moving wormholes with the canvases of my very breath. The smoothest of my skin lays a trail of Milky Ways, haze of universes within malty universes.

Breathing in glasses of galaxies, swimming in moments, molding novae with a simple gesture of forever.

Blanket of space infinitely spreads, engulfing our sun in its brilliant light. I sleep with you, all of creations. We inhale you, my love.

Day by Day

My motives are good, my movements are slow, but my rebel chaotic emotions have taken refuge in the center of every thought, which resides in my psychological mind patterns. The gears of an automatic system...

Autopilot is an unending energy within that shape of your uncut breath. Autopilot of the mind endless gathers thoughts that continue seeping into you. Out of me into truth. I spilled over your tongue, and my words grew as I delivered the bouquet of their meanings to you.

Swallow it as it burns my throat, as it upset my stomach and burns my heart. I spit it out while falling into the pool of their bitterness. I drowned and remanifested as a merman, an endowment of a mermaid.

Soon to be enslaved—become the best man, become the maid! A century has passed. I may have received a pay, a mental slave, a different stage! You're my Muppet, and my awareness state of self is the puppeteer. I own you, DAY BY DAY!

Watch

Watch me correlate with this moment that I take, rushing through my history and my understanding of late! The alarm bell rang. I walked through; my life has begun. Conceived has come, and she smiles at me.

Ripped into rigid decaying flesh of a caring hand. The tick, tick, tick has vanished! Gone! They're no longer here. Their gears have completely ceased to operate! I put my emotion, an extension of myself in action.

I took place in the same place where they were filming a movie, a theater in motion. I couldn't regret it, but I rewrote it, yet I couldn't go back! I lost track of time poachers. I wrote my moments; I wrote my journals; I wrote my love beyond the roads, but the gears wouldn't rewind to the moment I forgot to ship this fine wine. My mind began to frantically beat as my heart tended to my emotions like the string to a violin. I mentally erupted and made love with the tunes of my heart.

Beautiful Place

Do you know where the most beautiful place in the world is? That place! It includes silence...

The most beautiful place in the world possesses the knowing of silence. The most beautiful place in the world is where we live!

In between, inside of this phase of mirroring moments, this second, in between each breath! The most beautiful place in this world and outside of it is the in betweens—the titles that we create and hide in.

The most beautiful place in this world is in between the titles we create and that we hide in. The space in between is our creation birth; you see we live in between sparks! We live in between moments; we live in between seconds; and we live in between existence, for what lied within was a moment that recreated itself.

We are the entanglements, we are the strings, we are the mergers, we are the ignitions, we are the flames, we are everything that is warm, and we are everything that can ever be. See, everything that ever-be is in between, and in between is where we are. Where we are is where we live!

We give birth to a stream of screams, to anxiety, and to stress (a losing understanding), and to life, and to comprehension, and what we couldn't comprehend was due to our physical beings.

This organ, this mind sounds like a beautiful organ, the tool we used to create beautiful vibrations, which we are! That which we feast on each and every season, each and every yawn. I couldn't wake up in the morning without the smell of coffee beans, something that was grown from the earth.

Mother, father, and stability equal out a mother catastrophic mangles with inaccuracy, riddle with equilibrium falling, par to par. I can't keep balance of the heart, so the world will taste my fears and will understand my rage. But again who would be around to write it? If I was to ever have a helping hand… Magic and understanding, experience and exceptions!

The most beautiful place in the world is the one that we cannot hold; the most beautiful place in the world is inside ourselves.

Water Rain

S tand there. I see my feathers, but I don't see affection. I stand on the rain and look down. I see the simmer, the simmer of reflections staring back at me, a shadow of my former self. I like those kicks! Nice blue and white, just the way I like...

I love this weather, however no one can see me. They are always captured by my outer exterior, my physical AW! Therefore, losing trace of me. Into my visible, I saw thoughts!

I walk on this earth and I see the reflection of myself through the marrows of waterfalls. Make a wish, for no one can see me there, too entranced with the other world. Nice sneakers though!

It's a link; I wish that I could flip it! Let the marrow world reflect me, and let the inner world reflect what they cannot see. I'll be gone with the rain when sun yawns.

So Got This

I see the shoreline. I see her naval. Her print is so alluring; it's intoxication, so tempting! I'm on my path. The road is clear, resembling a still reflection. I'm seeing things! Those x pills and mollys have me sweating out Rémy Martin. I'm who-listing! But I know I'm near.

The white and black pavement, the road path and the cement, the review marrow is fill with crows and caskets. In front of me are multiple dimensions of possibilities simmering into now, forming buds that will transcend me before me.

I'm traveling what's behind and gaining that which I cannot see—yet since! I've received a bullet burial in my mind and had the cells digest through my thoughts, while they roll of my tongue and out of my mouth. They decorated the moon eyes with glowing craters.

My mood changes, revealing dripping blood white, trickling down my stain—black! I have collar creases, collar stripes…Why don't you understand that the pain is unbearable, describable, destructible? You tell me. Was I meant to carry this on the side-pavement?

I'm conjuring from a different perspective in the barrel of snow. I look outward to meet the sun under the sun, flickering in the crystallized air. I see the play fall in slow motion. The drizzle took the main role and brought the movie home. I will live here, or I want to stay forever...

Who? Why couldn't I remain?

I look down onto earth and seen what humanity created. Here is my spaceship. I am being monitored. What marvels of creations we have released onto this world! We have come so far only to destroy ourselves. Can this be the meaning of misery?

I lay there sexily. Kiss my navel. I'm a so intrigued by you. My hands are in praying form. Let's begin a Sutra with your plum-clover on my tongue. Let the words begin to waver as swiftly as the morning breaks. I stand there. Let this world course its bonds into a beautiful truth.

I am but a tool looking to shape our hearts. For the one we laid was now only a scattered mist of its former self. No matter how much of a menace I've become or how insane that I've become my voice will be heard. Mentally departed never need leave thoughts. I uplifted my stature with a robe shaping my form. My head inflated strings for legs.

You called me a moon man. The definite escaped me. Let me be the devastation. Bat around my neck. I'm not into paltry or animal cruelty, but when the night sky steps down, my fangs comes out. I will be our optical illusion. What you seen is not what you've gained. Take several moments, and look a tad closer. It will reveal itself. When you can finally see self, you will understand.

Unexpected

Unexpectedly it happened! The balloon burst, and blood-rain formed my tears. My uncertainties and my fears spilled out of me.

I was left there to die! My emotions pulled the trigger. My mind exploded! And I was misconfigured; I wasn't the same inside. I couldn't cry! My head became numb, my tongue became lifeless, my breath became suffocation, my life became death, and my death became my home.

I built according to my despair; I ate according to the love that I lost, so fragile when I was lifted, apart I was torn.

Separated in many sequences, I became mere fragments of my former self. My emotions. My love was no longer what it was, no longer what I had, no longer what I have.

What was left replicated a poor understanding of what I thought! And what I thought was a memory of a trophy that was made out of my own chards of broken dreams. Yet what kept it up was my will of a reality!

What took it away was her tainted love of immoralities she claimed for me. What brought it back was my love for me!

For at the end I saved me. At the end I used the broken pieces to create paradise! The utopia of my life...

I will be your sun; I will be your light; I will be the day when love enters your world; I will be the rose that sprouts out of pain; I'll be the garden that despair tends to; and I'll be your heart that cannot chatter.

We and I, you! And the world outside of this life is the meaning of my love, but let me rephrase it for you. If I can in one way, it will be this...

I am what you allow; what you allow is not who I am! What I've become is what I have molded. What I molded was my heart and soul, for I have built it outside of moments further then pain. It was reformed in between love and creation hands.

Old-Time

Watch me correlate with this moment that I take, rushing through my history and my understanding of late! The alarm bell rang. I walked through the fields. My life has begun! Birth has come; she smiles at me.

Broken and in disarray, the ticks, ticks are no longer noticeable; the gears have ceased to operate. I put my will in action and took my place. A motion picture played a movie theater in motion, but I rewrote it, yet I couldn't go back!

I lost track of time, run away nine. BANG! BANG! These lines formed a bloody massages. You will find a hollow point at the end of the puddle. Use it for your engagement. Bloody Mary, hail Mercy, see me in that written, rewritten Maserati!

I wrote my moments; I wrote my journals; I wrote my love beyond the road and into the heart of your rose, but the gears wouldn't rewind to the moment that escapes me, eludes me! I begin to whine. My mind begins to beat franticly as my dreams spill onto reality's dusty coach of a collection. This is what they called an old timers' celebration.

Hurt of You

Torn apart, shredded, turned to ashes. The flames crinkled the sounds, a flicker of light taken by the wind for a dance around the world home. Buried deeply, she ate me whole! I passed through her as she pushed me out inch by inch, moment by moment, releasing me through her bowels.

Falling fast, pulling gravities, curtains—dragging them through the mud and dust. The emotions cling to me! The pain rains. I took the sky flight and let the jet fuels sprinkle out the destinations of my falling heart.

That I had sprinkled the world with the rain of my broken emotions and used the broken pieces to build a home of lost memories and hopes! Then my joy would be in life's…bed!
Just waiting for my soulful melodies.

Took the pain of destruction and painted my inner room gloomy gray, picked up my saxophone and played with the blues while it changed views with green, allowing the grasses to move to the symphony of my mood.

Turn into staircases and climb up to the moon. Reach there by daylight, set there, and watch the world flicker in and out of existence, crumbling down with every exit it takes. Undoubtedly it has become what you call days, which in return enter into forever!

Encaged within my heart, I couldn't break free; I couldn't breathe! But I found a way. I found a place that was made specifically for me, for the damned. Who knew my own strength and compassion would've come alive and devoured me whole? Good night.

Good

I'm floating in my dreams. I'm floating in my bed. My bed is floating in my dreams. Outside I'm asleep; inside I'm lifeless. Flickers of me like day and night, grounds of night and day, black and white.

Star light, star lit—now who's scarlet? It turns into gray and black, less than the item is alone, the bucket that sails alone with the umbrella flipped upside down. This is better than another rain, another ring.

So we stand in the glister of days and see the resemblance as we age, but the world can't see us! For we have yet to arrive, yet these are the moments to come. A tide of concussion brings you to the foreground of your subconscious. I urge you to be cautious as I sever our unbreakable ordeal. So it has been ordain; I and you have gain. These are the games we entertain.

Captured Love

Just want you to know: the way you tame love is by releasing it, by completely letting it free! The way you tame love is not by commanding it! It's not by demanding it; it's not by control!

The way you tame love is with an invisible leash, and this leash is constructed with all the meanings of freedom. It doesn't restrain love; it doesn't bind love! It lets existence itself be the area where love resides.

The way you tame love is by you loving infinitely, while allowing that love which abides in another to be free! In this fashion love will be drawn to you, love will embrace you and protect you. Love will completely cloak you, embody you!

This my love, my friend, is the way you tame unconditional love. For the mere description of tame is but an eclipse you must walk through in order to claim clarity to the meaning of love, my dear.

It is unconstrained, fateful, and pure; it is all these things. It is the way she came, he came, to love each other, to love you! I love you, as friends to friends, lovers to lovers, honor to honor, and joy to joy—all of this under an umbrella coated with love, simply dancing in the spectacle of the wind, freedom of love.

My Photography

Romance, love, candlelight, lovemaking! I was conceived, and I was being released from my home of a darkroom. Cozy and warm, I saw light rocking back and forth. The room spun. I breathed in.

A feeling of a love so strong that it can only be borne by love from one plain of reality to another, land to a brother, a hug for one another. I swerved uncontrollably as I caught a fever. Tears flooded my face; their trail warmed my skin. I lived again.

Carry to guidance a leader's stance. Siblings follow; I'm a brother at hand. Reach our destination. Release and reach. Cruise, soothing as I paved the wrinkles of the ocean until it bared me a home of ripe, hanging mangos—tasting, slicing, dripping on my tongue! It felt so refreshing, so quenching.

I grew from one state to another. I grew! I lost my mother. I grew! Hurt and betrayed, marriage, married you, decayed, forever you, rotten! Farewell to you, poetically unjust, emotionally bound. I am the construction of all these metabolic experiences.

I breathe you and exhale art, stich words of life's pure silence in order to evoke the emotions of a celestial god out of you! I am a captured moment expert; you may call me photography! I love every moment: street views, love's views, and understanding these perceptions of you. For these reflections are me, mirroring me!

I see it in the rearview. I see it behind you. I can see it in the reflections of streams, puddles of me! You are kind, loveable, understanding. I am kind, loveable, and understanding…

I am the friendship of compassion. I am the advocate of love, and my heart along with my testimony is my gift to you! I am poetry, I am divine, I am photography, so follow me.

All

I remember when tattoos were ten dollars and ladies were free. Piercings were five dollars back in my day. I wasn't free! Ladies, don't fight over me, please! Pulling your blond, black hair, your blouse falling, your skirt falling, pulling off that sexy...

Where's my hand? Blow pop me. Damn, babe. Lie flat down. You grind; I love that! The chamber looks clean. Girl!!! I'll fire you up like that aftermath of the gun powder off that trigger.

Tie your legs up with chains. tie you up, suspend you in the air and eat you bare! Drinking that tattoo body, labels for me. Lie yourself on the table for me. You smell the same, perfume beautiful. You're perfect just the same.

Let me lick you. I like your smirk. You tell me you're not ashamed, so I change things, reshape things. I promise you bitch, after tonight! You will never be the same. Purple Kush, blue bud—hold up!

I crave a love so deep that the ocean would be insecurely jealous and the end of time would become our home. I crave a love so vast that we become extensions of space itself, so close your eyes and have me while I devour your entrance, your noble place.

I'm your inside tsunami, super suction like salami, babe, but fresher than life. There's meaning between you and I. Let the flowers bloom. Let me tap into the portal of forever and bear witness to what comes out, what define my equator, meaning my creator.

Family of love seeks representation. Full of temptations, so last breath. A home made out of mushrooms, fields of weeds, blows, blows, marking the moment of its blossoming.

My Fashion

I create devastation with my words. Wrap it around the world; wrap it around yours! Artistic bond, I am profound. Landed onto these moments of now creating artistic words, cerebellum complete control...

Cerebral cortex! The grids, the platform of our departure home, four rooms of my own hold my emotions along with my heroic action and store my words in that provided place, leaving my sight with the doors wide open. Can you feel the pressure of my touch? Hear me and remember you're welcome as you please, brain list.

Let me enter into you, and let me remain there. Let me camp there, bonfire. Every second let my words be what ignite the blaze of sparks. See your dome release and relate. I am the artistic foundations of the cathedral, since the ancient wisdoms imprinted in my words, see them in my features.

My smirks disguises and describes all that is in one glimpse. The awareness that I breathe will soothe you, will allow you to live.

A Rare Maiden

It was between her thighs, whispers between my lips, to the canvas of her undergarments. I sense a breeze, a cold wind traveling down my spine. I'm so levitating; I'm so suspended in the flood of her love portrait, resembling the collage of her ecstasy emotion.

I am gravitation-less. I twinkle my jester. She's wet beneath me, leaving her scent and stain on me, my baby couch! Oh, this breeze! Her legs, her hair, her lips, her smile…flutter in the air like a multitude of pollen in the atmosphere of her—so wild and majestically free, magically hovering in bliss.

Oh! Woman you're so sexy. Take that drape of a dress off of you. Pledge your heart to me. Glide over to me. Hover over my ego, my ambitions. Drool all over me and swallow me. I'm your high-grade, sexually! You're grade A, a rare maiden you are, a wife for sure! My maiden, devious allure. Yes! A devil-less allure. I smell the black and white roses, the fragrance of her plum rolling off my tongue.

Path to You

Walking through a land of forest and dark into midseparation, mist and light, midsunrise; my path is gloomy. The cracks that course through the leaves beneath my feet warm me! My heart is captured by my fear and held hostage from my joy, and I move forward.

For I am the answer, for I am of you! Beautiful trees of grim leave stems of him and reach out for me, for I am you. Let me travel where you cannot and hold what you cannot hold. In return, nurture me where I cannot live, shelter me where I cannot hide, and let us love and interlace into the depths of morning light, the sign of life!

Let the melodies of our binding, in our union capture our moments. We dreamt of this; this is our meadow, my memento to you!

In Me

I do! And I want to…I lay here and I do ponder about things: how I want us to be, how I would like your smile to remain perfectly framed on your gentle face like a picture that cannot decay. Oh! How I wish I could have it frozen there, where existence doesn't interfere with it.

For it is the most beautiful feature I've ever seen within you! What I'm trying to say is that I love you, and that I can accomplish anything! I can do anything, because there will be nothing too high, too great that can restrain me from accomplishing these things for the sake of we.

But babe, my love, I won't tell you that I need you, but babe, when I tell you, "I need you!" I need you to release these floodgates of possibilities that lie within me to such an extent that I take you to different horizons, different freedoms of intellectually elevated realities.

I want to see us on cruises just because. I just want us to be rude and be bold just because. I would love us to stare onto the rubies of love and bear witness to the different orchestras of our shattered shards of love, reflected back into us.

And with the light of the sun enlisting the light within us, filling us with feelings of heart beats. We swallow it into a lovely kiss. Nothing you can do is not beautiful. Even your flaws are the most beautiful things I've ever seen.

It's like staring at a staircase of roses until they bloom into a bed of roses, and there I will take you and lie with you and make love to you and tell you lies that I cannot make it, so that you can realize that I already have, because you were with me every. step. of. the. way. Our dreams, my dreams. I have everything you want inside of me; it's yours for the taking.

Midnight Train

The midnight train! Route to nowhere: the midday train. Route to possibilities: the night train crashed into the eerie mist of 1820! My grandpa was there; he was an old fella! Didn't really have a good ear for soothing melodies or a feel for the weather for that matter...

The midnight train to nowhere, the nightshift train to somewhere, the sun train, the pole came falling down, bloody share, scream alarms! Imbalance appeared with no alarm, but snow fell in the violent street as it screamed "which of who is true."

What a fierce fire of brave, a young maiden appeared. Her gestures were calm. The moon glistered over her hair, reflecting the night light into moonlight my vibrating my very being.

Grow in me this moment. Defeat was of no man. I created this word, this label. I took their voice away, back in the table of 1820. Sweet tales of honey, gravestone, and money.

Cry

I went deeper. Made her soul cry my name before I could even reach her, before I could even taste her lips! I told her stories with the orchestra gestures of my hands. I entered her mind with but a gaze and opened the floodgates into places she didn't even know existed. Because I wanted her to know!

I gave her every secret, opened her to spaces she's never been and took her to pathways that were paved by god! Oceans were made out of the tears of our lovemaking, nurturing the grassland of our ancestors.

She needs me to dive into her deeply! I touched her; I caressed every portion of her, until she reached the moment of her childbirth. I made her body travel backward; I made her heart beat in between our breaths as her love flowed forward.

Creating an incredible song of never-ending bliss and pure happiness. It baffled me, left me without words, made her hit notes that brought peace to humanity. We were put whole again; I merged her into me again.

Awaiting Love

If I can live, then you have loved me! If I wake up in your arms again, then I have loved you in my dreams. If I fall asleep, then you have captured my heart in both worlds.

My Home

On my red, pink, orange and white, peach pink, yellow bloom! My case on the other hand, a hazy morning sun, blaze on the light pole, the grain of pebbles below, gouge my imprint into the fog.

Trees flapping and clapping with the sway and command of the wind. Go for whatever makes you happy. It's a journey she in barked on and that I took for my home, leaving her all alone in her newfound home.

Breathe Me

Fell from the sky and used the plane as my diving board; I noticed it cried! Caught the rain from its teardrops. I fell from the ocean with an ice block. Frozen cold, I craved and I carved my cold heart.

Threw it in the air as it split like dry leaves, transformed into a Marine! Life-like creature trapped in the barrel in my heart...It beats antifreeze, it beats ice through my veins, and it feeds the tree of light. I bit and ate myself through the foggy mirror. It's lightning, light effects transport me into my state of now only, to meet my reflection.

I melt before myself and drip beneath the soil, transforming into an ogre. So beautiful. I climbed the clouds and slept in stars while bashing in the sun. I lived in the footsteps of your kindhearted miles.

I spent my moments on the creases of your lips. I spent my life at the tip of your love. I died with your love! So without any reasonable doubt, I took that out of you and never despised you, my Nubian queen! So please breathe me, breathe me...

Befouled You

Take my pain and screw it deeply beneath my skull, beyond what you call my mind, to the seat of my emotions. Let my agony drown, gasping for relief. Let it sink, let it die slowly so that I can have peace.

Tears drop down my face at the speed of molasses, forming my glasses, which were given to me at the end of my classes. For I cannot see precisely as they did; my eyes created the vulture.

I peeled their heart with the richness of my words, with the scalpel of my vengeance. I was decapitated with my own pride and fell completely to the earth. The clouds stared down at me with their eyes of gray, forming thunderclouds to strike me before I lay dead!

Stumbled in between streets, pebbles, and chicks, because the double hour on the table doesn't reflip. The jaw dropping sticks; the barrel is hot! My revolver of a trigger hand is all so involved.

I'll bakery grave you, so enjoy your gravy! I befouled you. Bow to your knees and unfold your fear and let your dreams and hopes take to the world like butterflies in winter. I know it's rare…BANG!!! I see its halo.

Perfect Face

A perfect face, a perfect place, a perfect moment describing all of your elegances and extravagances took me for a trip from which I couldn't return. Your smiles, your gestures, your futures got me painting pictures, memories!

My culture, your structure. You got me completely wrapped around you, like a perfect orchestra! I was lost in you; you've taken me! Your stride along with those pearly whites; your grace—your ulterior, exterior—captivated me in all areas.

I was under your spell. I was bound by you, living in your atmosphere, rotating around you. I gravitated toward you. You see! You're able to cast love spells just by glance. I said "I do," and laid my pillow next to you.

Share my days with you! Coffee cup, mango joy, trips here and there—the full affair! I kiss you, mix with you, only to enter you and notice something terribly wrong with you. The worst nightmares came to flesh in her flesh. You see, your inner was destructible.

You exploded me and ripped me apart limb by limb. Cannibalism, a living hell! You were terror. My heart broke apart. I woke up in sweats, drenched! A nightmare between beauty and life. I flew without a parachute. I wish I'd never met you.

Our Mess

It's quiet right now and my thoughts are loud. Tossed and turned while the lights were out. Had a dream that the gorilla ripped your head off.

Now my heart thumps deep down inside my chest wondering if you're at rest! Are you alone?

The world would have to see you dead in order for you to see the world. The world would have to see you dead in order for you to see the world...

For this is when you're truly alive: with the truth of life as your prize. Because I think I'm failing this test of our mess, which we created! Do your best and stay blessed!

My Very Own

Childlike-spoiled bottle, spilled milk cry like an infant, ingrown, immature, wants the world for his own, but unpin point destination. Friends... alone! Claim the world for his home but without understanding, without comprehension.

He let his home fall apart to tremble, to fade. Trees and lift. Fall has faded. Yet he stands tall, stands tall like a child without a home, like everything came crumbling down—a bottle in hand!

We're his friends; we're his home. I'm afraid that he's all alone simply because of all his personal personalities: his attributes, his stubbornness, his ignorance. But at the end of the day, it will take a creator's intervention to bring him back home. Only then will he have a friend to call his very own.

RobDade

RobDade—day and night, night and day—not a blanket, not a slate! Bring dreams into reality, your concept to standard point of view. 1080p! My prospective view. This is Miami city where the sunrise and no one sleeps.

Under my eyes, RobDade! The county, Miami Dade, where you work all night and work all day. Truth and honor to friends, loyalty is must, bitch third, not second, they aren't even worth it!

RobDade, embodiment of successes. Truth and honor rules through the society of this undercover direction of directors. DP, you hear me? Let my work echo throughout the years, way before I'm gone, because you will always remember that I'm ROBDADE. My work speaks for itself—always on play!

Masquerade

I don't understand! Asking the structure of myself: within self, why? Electrical impulses firing back and forth. My synapses are blazed. My neurons are responding. No answer is given…

I believe that if you're pure, then pureness will take hold of your life. I believe if you're pure, joy will flood your life. And I believe if you're joyful, then pureness will flood your joy. But I ask myself why?

You said that you love me, but it's just joy in a masquerade! Of decay and hate, a euphoria of a poison, tailored to destroy me—and for every time I take you in! You affect my heart, and it explodes.

Well refined spikes penetrate every inch of my heart, leaving nothing in their wake but a black hole of complete despair. It replays and again I mend you, and again you unmend yourself, and again I take her back, and again it happens.

It happens, but this time the masquerade of a joyful hate, a joyful love, has redefined itself, more importantly to destroy me. My heart wasn't enough. The black oboist wasn't enough! It traveled throughout your whole being.

Entities that create me—joy, hope, love, and faithfulness—affected my will from being discouraged and saved me from being eaten up alive! You have no mercy; you feed off my kindness.

You feed off my neglects to harm! You feed off my childlike innocence. You burrowed deeply into my psyche and tried to rip out my equilibrium of peace, but I stood steadfast, and I was one with all. I gathered my strength through all and was able to see you!

The anomaly in my life, the thorn against the river of joy, the world of peace, the pureness of me—I see you! Trying to pierce through me, you won't defeat me! Because I don't believe in this image I see, this plague, you, are beneath me, because, my love, my joy and my pureness are not reachable by the likes of you.

Monkey Cage

Breaking light—sunray—fills my darkness, fills the spaces, and raised my mind. Cage down to these four walls, brick walls! I hear the chatters; I hear the cling. Creating sparks revived me; a ray of light absorbed me.

Floating ever so gently in midair, her form, her design—WILD! My wings were plucked, floating to an undetermined destination, free as self! The source of great—alone I fall, so gently I sleep.

Once encaged monkey beast! Pull out my banana on you—monkey piece! Let these tones float to towers to towers. Hear my tones: piano to guitars, gray clouds, alpha towers. I bathe and bask in these glorious moments of cowards.

I sleep in the bed of seas. Umbrellas hold my seat, bucket floating. I'm falling, sinking; my bed is merged and immersed in the sea. Brownwood, I can smell it, you see! Games I play: water lamps, I type my story for the next to hear me.

My home captures moments—photography! Bark as loud as you can. I got trees behind me! Home image, memories captured, smiles for a lifetime. I remember my mother...father, sister. How we grew with one another...

This house is a photography memory, photo memory. I can understand you; can you hear me? I can taste you. Your legs of a ballerina stretch so nicely on my back. Me in between your lips licking your excitement from my lips—reflection of me tasting you.

I just want you! I want you to just trickle down into my life, into my spine, and exit out of my ecstasy, out of my orgasm. Mouth to mouth, resuscitate me and give me life! Under your pussy mistletoe, ringa bell, ringa bell. What a beautiful bell you are, my Elizabeth; how I love you so! Monkey ammo—BANG!!!

Wisdom of Now

In this place, you've sustained me. You provided me! I gave to you by day; you took from me by night. Whereon my psyche, whereon my mind, whereon my pride drifts off onto a merger. I remember we met her before our murders.

Mother always knew. Lost count of a systematic calculation. I gave you by day; you took by night—an imbalance of dim to bright. I was starving; you feasted. You starved; I feasted. I lost my balance; you ate my feet. All that was left was a cavity of a tooth containing the wisdom that we gained.

Now

Float on a cosmic peninsula to unknown terrains, to unknown meadows. As you sleep in my world of dreams, as I float on top of your strings, these cosmos float! These cosmic waves, these cosmic ripples, are monumental mementos.

Tokens to my emotions that overflooded when you touched, caressed, and lingered your voice upon my chest. Open this treasure chest of gold that has been buried beneath known words: known love, known divines, known mystical events.

I am…I swim in the heaven in us! I am, you are, we are miracle inventions of now.

Earth, Thank You

These four walls are cold. My chair, my stool, these painting are cold. These four walls are cold. These floors are cold. These paintings are warm.

I live in a place that soaks me and strings me up to dry, but I use my gift to survive.

Hanging by my kind heart against the wall like a wet cloth, I guarantee you that my stomach is the closed door to your half sandwich, the dishes that weren't cleaned, the mind that wasn't even rewound.

I reconstructed and recreated my fireplace.

They say it didn't exist, but just the mere sight of it is keeping my heart warm, my flesh alive, my breath deep, and my senses—you see! What's keeping me alive is the light in me, so please let me enlighten you.

There is no feat that you cannot achieve; there's nothing that you cannot gain, contemplate, and retain. Rebuild it and break it down, destroy it! It was never intangible, but for everything that came before, you were always nothing less but incredible.

Go forth and create the world without the image you thought of or that you brought, but within the fashion in which they thought, but who's they? It's you! So I have to thank you for giving birth to me and allowing me to live on your wind and water. Therefore, Earth, I thank you, forever, furthermore.

Lotus Flower

A secret garden, a secret entity, a sacred place: a wooden tree filled with the blossoming roses of lotus flowers. As refreshing as you are. Remarkable. You are a smile that blossoms, a nectar that is the richness of sweet!

Let me relive these moments on top of your petals the sun has absorbed. I have grown and tasted all your meanings along with their understandings. Cradle me into the moment and watch life through the reflection of your eyes. You watch life through my facial expressions of surprise.

We are lotus flowers, secret to one another, flowering together. Angels, fathers, mothers, sisters to one another. My love, you are my lotus flower, and I am your nectar.

Frost

It's truly a vague comparison of you in the white and black snow and that shadow of you. Your beautiful dress torn from the ankles up. Your hair is long and dark as night. This is truly a pale likeness of you.

A drench snow. A complexion as wonderful and unspoken for. A complexity as the vastness of ember-stars that lives within you, we and me, lost in the wilderness of your euphoria, inhale the mist of my high and exhale life!

Really! A dreary image of you. I would love to hold you, soak you into my mirage, bathe you within my imagination. Let me coat your flesh with the vapors of my excitement as I lick the cold out of you and bring warmth along with its cradle of life into we.

My Son

The stillness of my emotions displays my devotion. The stillness of my ocean showcases the depths of my skies. I'm afraid of the rain.

I'm braver when I run. Fall into a runt of a rut just to end up climbing out of trunks. Ledges and bridges, I burn! So please feel my stillness of heart's.

For they reflect my concerns. Bright as the sun, bright as the newborn, back and forth, the carriage, something I truly cherish, a gift that is truly full of abundance. I thank you for my son!

Into One

In the moment of this second, in the second of this moment, I am lost, I am found, I am continued, and I am forever. I began to write this rumor, this mystery. In the animal eyes, I see into you; I am restored.

All along these moments, we're rearranged in the frame of reflections. Flashes of me, resembling me...I was devoured before I even awakened, a mystery of love—carnivore! We are now one.

Universe Inside

Have the universe in my mouth! Have it reshaped and reformed, and have it redeliver itself into many elements of our birth. Let the universe tongue role out my mouth—the synchronicity of our union, of our correlation.

Watch the solar system of misplaced relativity of information, watch the constellation of my belt around the archangel Jabril's wings. Power and dreams, hopes and heart, awaken from the slumber of our creativity.

We have created God among gods, cathedral upon cathedral; the aftermath has truly emerged as the masterpiece of humanity's destructive ideology. Infinite my words, bind to you written in words that are stone to you. Thrown in, too, the wrinkles of my heart. It barely moved a single beat.

Time & Space

I learn how to walk. I learn how to eat space and time so that we can meet! I learn how to swallow and gulp those memories so that I can relive them inside of you. I walk the bridges of cemeteries so that I can close the gap between our histories.

I hold you close to my heart, so you can always reach me! I know that everything that is now will be yours and will be mine. I can't forget about today because I'm creating it as you follow me.

Cradle me in your arms, and I will allow my love to cradle you all along. You see, because I learn to eat time and space so that we can meet. I mean, I grew strong with patience and understanding!

I always wanted to make you happy. I smiled in your face and at the moments we had. We carried baseball bats, flew kites, and just remembered the wild nights. I just wanted you to know that lying next to you and waking up next to you is one among my infinite memories that I cannot forget nor release!

So please teach me how to give birth to the love that I have forgotten. Teach me how to give birth to my pain. Teach me how to eat your memories, and I'll teach you how to eat my moments and sprinkle them with stardust, because the romance that cradles in time and space lingers in my mouth and drenches my tongue and fulfills my entire essence.

It brought me to a stop of red and green lights, joy and love the building of skyscrapers. I built sketches with the skies cast aside. I just want you to know that I love it when we are outside—catch that, outside—and you have me forever. Just remember me. I will always relieve you, because I need to find you. Reach every square corner of life, because I need to find you, you see! These memories need you, so I swallow time and space to meet you.

Drawers

Iopen the drawers to your heart, the cabinets to your mind, the understanding of your body in mind. Soulfully you lay. I reach out to you so gracefully and tenderly. I'm exposed to you! Pull out those wrinkles of clothing in my heart that I have worn over and over again.

I know they are indecent. I know they are tainted, but here! Take them and hang them for me, wash them for me, clean them for me. I slowly reveal to you what's within my cabinets. My borders are revealed.

Follow me and repaint me. Provide me with a different combination, a different sequence of patterns as my hair is unleashed onto my back and I fall asleep on top of your mind. I climbed…

These mountain peaks. I fall, I fold. And hopes that I am reclaimed, recleansed, reclenched by your hands! I see all these through the structure of your lies. The sadness in your eyes and the way sleep falls into you at night.

I will wear all the clothing of your emotions so proudly that I will create a scent that our life will forever be stained with!

So wherever you may linger your vision, whatever you may smell, wherever you are, know that I am the clothing inside of you. I am these emotions that you wear, the belts and the garments. I am proud to be me! I am proud to be you! And I thank you for this evening. I thank you for this evening! Thank you for purchasing me! I am your antique! I am your brand. Thank you, thank you!

I Don't Know Truth

I'm a doodle. I'm being created with each stroke, each gesture, and with every electrical thought, I become more alive. The form of a cube attaches with sight, smell, but I'm missing an eye.

Something itches! I see roots on top of my tools, my station! A dandelion appears; she's my dandelion on the rooftop of my stool of my tool. Blur my vision with multiple sketches and strokes.

I'm a sketch inside of a stroke, black and white penmanship, implantation, implementation. There's nothing to say...add to the situation. I'm stuck in this cube where you can only see a quarter of me, but I'm still with you.

It's cold so I cover that half of you. I belong to all of them! Long ago, I stood all alone. Eerie vision, ill reflection, your preference, your perception. The night was haze glistering with darkness, a glacier of harmless harmony soothing as I stood still as the dark moon, revealing my true state.

I'm correlated with earth, alien to most, alien to this earlier structure, earlier then her. Phase me away from now like a puppeteer, a vessel without any entity of stars.

I ripped open her hand and crucified her denial on the walls of my heart and burned the edges of her screams, yet I care for the little demon inside, so there they go—the bending of crooked needles of my farewell.

My Mind

My mind is a labyrinth filled with mazes, and my thoughts' form is the embodiment of a Minotaur. Come deep and fall steep.

I will lead you into my secrets and let you fall asleep. I will devour you before you weep, before you wake from your sleep. So please, so please don't follow me.

Reach

The moment you let my hand go so that I could fly to the vast openness from where you came, you seemed to be lost to that notion! Let me bring forth out of you a new and profound you that has always been there waiting for a stimulation to vibrate your very being. Anything and everything is capable and in reach for you! Doors will open and doors will close in all to retain the very essence of your will and determination to become more than you are today!

I Am

I'm better than Edgar Allan Poe! I'm the prodigy of Maya Angelou. I don't know you enough to love you for the world, but I know you well enough to love you for myself.

Heathen Feet

Insecurities run toward it, fold after fold, time fold! I'm confused, yet I stand my ground. I'm about to be transformed into the ground, rebirthed into the Grim Reaper, without a soul, without thought.

I am here to be commanded! He rested her hand behind my back and gave orders one-handed. His grim. Her face. His nose. Her glare—scarf so high, business-minded, election stare—transforms my genuine thoughts, my innocence, into fears.

Fight, anger, and destruction among man of nations that I have no quarrel against. Brethren create divisions, and I have not begun to shed one tear. I carry a scythe!

They call it a rifle. I stood deep in a helmet. They call it a halo.

They transform many of my brethren, many of my sisters into enemies of life! I am the carrier and the disposable, but I went so far into these grand fields, landmines. There are explosions in my mind, and I can't begin to despair, because I call it forth with one single breath, with one single rotation of my scythe.

Recycle and recite these words: I am birthed into this world to rejoice in everything and everything, for I am everything! Everywhere is not controlled by another, but for it is controlled by greed.

Something has been preconceived, precollected, preconsumed—a disease infested within the womb. They are birthed with the notion to control. They feast on death; they feast upon agony. They're obese, with the belly of a beast! Their gluttony has no rest, has no feet!

Please gain stability. Let your awareness bring forth flesh to you. Let your understanding decay your scythe. Let your love bring sight. Let that helmet wither away. Let your back sprout out wings, because peace is what you are. Love is what we are. We'll dine in heaven's doors and let these heathens eat their own feet.

Perfect

We're perfect. We're more than a human being. I we are of the source, all of creation, space and existence itself.

Decorating Balloons

The elephant in the room grows louder and louder as it stomps around like an angry toddler, thrashing its head, knocking over furniture. You watch its destructive ways. Every day the elephant makes its presence known, trying to get the others in the room to move, to bend, to pay attention to it. The more it feels ignored, the louder it gets.

But wait, what was that? A mouse! Yes, a tiny little mouse is sitting in the corner of the room as this elephant grows louder and louder, thrashing its head. All along, the mouse is keeping quiet, staying still, waiting, and watching.

It's unsure if it should go or should it stay. The longer it stays, the louder the elephant becomes, to the point that it's unbearable. But the longer the mouse stays, the more it sees the elephant for what it really is: just a bully!

I don't like bullies decorating their action with an elaborate celebration filled with panic and anxiety balloons. The longer I stay in the room, the more I see. The more I see, the more at ease I become, for the elephant eventually falls asleep!

It was expensive. It drained its owners' emotional funds until he was no more—silent as a mouse! I held the prize in my mouth—gold and diamond emotions. I restored his emotional wealth. Stay clear free of the elephant's wrath, or you too will be lost in the depth of its emotional void.

Wildfire He Is

A natural substance you cannot contain. WILD cannot be restrained. Like the lion he is, he ROARS his name and shows his fangs.

Symbolism, symbolize, symbol of his flames. He is alive! You can fall into his haze, his gaze. It is contagious. It's very dangerous!

Like the quick yet elegant cheetah paws, he spreads quickly throughout the land, crackling. He can be your enemy or your friend, your confidant, your ally, your advocate.

He stands. His stance. See the day move into night. Hand in hand, he ceases the day! Carpe diem! He ROARS! WILDFIRE: his blazing courage strengthens me!

Ransom

The ransom to my happiness is all around me. If only I could see it! If only they could understand it!

Tried

The things that break my heart are the same things that make me smile. The things that create my tears are the same things that mend my heart. The world goes on, and the story ends.

Cover me with golden dust and rip out my diamond thoughts. I arose from the frost; it was cold when you spoke! This road, this path is the same thing. I was rewarded with resembling things that mend my broken heart.

You see! They live in between multiple moments, but they resemble my very home—the same as your very own—my broken heart of a home, yet it mends, and my smile renames the moment, because I have always tried.

I Am Perfect

I am perfect! I am not human; I am of unseen possibilities…

Position Queen

The utmost powerful position proclaimed to my queen is specifically aligned with me! Firmly, yet gently, she stands three steps behind me and holds her stance…to the left of me! She perceives what I cannot, while standing bold and brave from behind my shadows.

She counters any attacks before they breach or reach me. She's firm in her beliefs. She can see far from the east and equally from the west. Her penetration expands her concentration to the north and further south, four pillars underneath her cathedral! She performs with three to protect me and uses the other to defend me.

Three steps wide is my stance! I protect this king with the gestures of my hands.

I acknowledge your stance, my queen. Elegantly you dance in the beauty of my protection, as I stand resembling Poseidon with his trident at the helm. I am your king! You are of me, a reflection of my greatness, constantly reminding me, strengthening me. Assume the position!

Embrace Continuum

The moments may pass and your flesh may not last, but breath slowly and inhale deeply! Understand that your words carry force, power, and enlightenment, which resonate from within you! They will infuse the ones who carry a listening ear.

The echo of your voice delivers strength because it carries you! You were never truly your physical state, yet your dazzling flesh reflects of you, containing you! Be brave and carry on, for when you return to your home.

To that body you call your very own, know that you are that instrument that lit the ideals of many. In a room filled with the ones that will hear you, filled with the ones that will feed off of you! For you will live within them, a portion of you into forever.

They will become your body! They will become your limbs! They will walk, they will hear, they will speak—and the world will change at its great peak! You were the change. You were the momentum, and for this I thank you, for the days you've rocked back and forth in front of your porch.

Sincerely

A rouse this ocean out of me! As we lie here among these ponds of lilies, let our synchronicity with the universe correlate infinitely into the bed of our wonders. Let jealous Pluto sing disturbing notes of our distorted admirations.

We glide and sing. Awaiting the anticipation—paradox! The moment of penetration…Sip the ocean out of me so that we can preconceive the moment I gave birth to this new reality. As these ocean waves remain beneath me, we form our celestial dynasty. Royal, for I crave all of you! My uplifting emotions.

Erase my memories and embed yours; penetrate me deeply! Unleash me so that my ocean elixir can breach the threshold of my golden paradigm, releasing my mind-control completely under your command. My joy, my fulfillment, while I lie here on a lake of your memories.

Bare me the understanding of childbirth as I tinkle with excitement, and let my eyes dance perfectly with the sparkles of the stars, letting them soothe me and calm me as we lie on our ocean bed. I deeply crave this!

Soothe me with alibis of your melodies and leave me here. Leave me here so that I can submerge myself in these moments: memories, fragments, and mirages of my own divinity. Give to me the predestined birthplace of our maybes.

I'm entrenched here, from below to my hair. These ecstasies of moments, these thresholds of identification—it was you! This misty night, this mystical fright, I lay here this night in this creek as your ocean love surrounds me, and I wait until it drowns me, takes me! My breath is away. It was gone when you left me, sincerely!

Do You See?

What do you see in those eyes? I see the sadness, fear, gentleness, fragility; I see the beauty of a heart. What do you see in those eyes? I see love. What do you see in those eyes? I see myself. What do you see in those eyes? What do you see in yourself?

I see a willingness to continue. What do I see? I see: The vortex doorway into you! A home of self. A place where fear doesn't exist! What do I see? I see the hope of man without sight. What do I see? I see me, we, soul!

Who Are You?

Who are you? What are you? You then told me that who you are and what you are is energy and that you have become the reality that you have created.

What is your name? You then told me, "Nameless," but you're not that! You said no. I asked why. You replied, "It's a label."

What is a label?
A label is false identification. A label is created to keep you captive from your true self. Oh! What have you accomplished?
Nothing! For I am one of the same with everything!
Therefore, you have accomplished everything, for you are everything! So who are you?
Energy.
What are you?
The realities that I've created.
So what have you created?
Everything!
What do you do with everything?
I transform it into life.

Whose life?

My life, for the realities that I've created are my life!

How many lives can you create?

Multiple lives.

Why?

Because I know who I am!

Who are you?

Energy.

Oh! What are you?

The lives that I've created using the ability to create realities; now I have understanding, young awaken one! Use your awareness wisely, for it can very well become your casket of immortality.

The Devil May Smile

The devil may cry and heaven may fall, but my door will remain closed—far from all! Let my heartbeat collect the tones. Shivering in feet, I walk, breathe. You see the bravery within me. I read green, royal purple.

I stand still because the years fall on me like raining meteor showers. My origin is of your smiling particles, regularly folding and bending me, yet the stars flicker on and off just enough to capture your evil grin. Eat souls like heroes without flavor. I hear men cheer and women cheer louder! Birth a new… That's the ladder.

The devil may cry and heaven may fall, but my door will remain closed! They feast on my pain as if it were a dessert at a buffet—as if it were a feast! I give them thanksgiving leeches; I give them thanksgiving dreams. It broke their hearts, along with their screams.

Heaven crumbles and the devil's devastation spread throughout their realms: sculptures broken, death to dust—they fall! God may cry and The devil may smile, yet my doors will remain closed. I'm beyond Pandora's box. What lies within was created within: a manifestation of pain and grief deriving from love, a condition that was created within a paradigm of a mind, a paradox of destruction.

Can you see the darkness within these ancient moments? They are monuments of gifts disguised as joy, like Helen of Troy, truly a destruction of joy, but the devil may smile and God may cry. Heaven may fall, and hell may rise, but I will remain the same, with my eyes wise with sight and my heart closed. You don't have to wonder why; the evidence is in my disguise!

Entrenched Love

You fly through my mind every second! You fly through my mind every moment! Take the wingspan of a destination. You are planted deep inside my heart. You are the cavity that is called egoistic!

To me, you replay like a goldmine that doesn't exist! You are the oil fields; you are the toxins in my soul. I'm addicted to your voice; your patterns, your sexual nature are stitched into me like unterrain, an untraveled destination.

You're random! You have my mind calling god. I am in turmoil, and your gestures are strings to my harp; vibrations of every note are the answers to my downfall, for the love I have for you have fallen and risen over and over, so it obtained its own melody, and if you were to ever hear it, you would hear tragedy...

You would hear: A love so pure that God would come down and anoint us! A love so eradicated and full of destruction that the Devil would bless us! A heart so pure that he would sacrifice his happiness for you, for your pure reincarnation of self.

You see I love you so much that I destroy myself in hopes of rebuilding myself, but you stand in my way to destroy me, yet at the same time say you adore me and love me. I hate these things! Yet it's a passion in which I have no restraint; therefore, I cry with the hope of strings wrapped around my heart and into my mind, so they can coexist, one moment after the other for if not, I will surly lose this egoistic mind of mine—thus freely fleeing to the world that I can coldly call my own.

You have not shown true compassion, for I know of it, I taste of it, and I can smell of it! To understand what you've done is to cease and let be! But you fight so savagely, so forcefully, so demandingly! Yet you don't hear your voice.

Your general nature is against the general master; you treat me as if I'm your peasant, as if I'm your bitch and you're the omega, but you can't see the concepts of my thoughts and why they remain so still.

So stoned, so embedded in my mind that you won't be able to understand the language that it weaves, yet you cry as if you do! Banding me to the furthest and deepest region of your hatred-heart for me. Look me daintily in my eyes and lie to me. I was never your fool; I just pretend to be!

How do I feel? I feel like passages in my life infused with something that can't be removed. You take me and draw me in like a beautiful painting. I'm under your canvas, but I feel like I'm decaying underneath you.

You could care less for me, because I'm starving, but you give 3fs, but you complain about your cooking. You ignore me, but you say you love me! You cause me pain and strife, but you say you love me! You cause me freedom, yet you say you're in love with me! You take from me, yet you say you're in love with me! You gave me no successor to the throne, yet you say you're in love with me! You foiled my success, yet you say you're in love with me!

I don't know what your meaning of love is, but if it is this, then you have killed me before I could show you, before I could teach you how to truly love, how I love you! Now you try to resuscitate me with the love you learned to love back, a tool that has been imbedded in you by God! Hoping that it's enough to call me forth into your arms again, for forcefully you attempt, and forcefully I am being buried deeply further away.

You reach out your hand, and I have none to reach back! But you complain and give me no glory for what I've sacrificed on your behalf. You don't see the hand that I played. You call me blasphemy. You erase me while looking down on me with a petty gaze, with your insulting thoughts, in hope that I have lost my days. I'm insane, you proclaimed! While avoiding any type of blame, you feel pain for the pain you have inflicted. What sense does it make? What logic does it carry? What strength does it hold? You're insane! For your actions sing the truth, for I am the conscience that speak righteousness back into you.

Sick and tired of this role, I release myself onto the road of destiny. I will grow and bear my wings and leave you be, for you have not breathed me success or showed me lessons that would strengthen my core.

You take away and you break me, but claim to want more! Do you truly seek my happiness? Or is it a path to satisfy your never-ending hunger for destruction of another.

You

If you have something like that in your heart, how do you expect the world to see you?

Labyrinth of Letters

Madly in love with your flavor of honey that guards the rims of your soul! I understand this moment of gratification. We take our place next to the Pope. I stand radiating our hopes, surpassing man's construction of heaven—you call this the Vatican!

Spare me all of this and see me sit on my throne. I love these theaters of chambers we remodeled after our plays, for they remind me of Rome.

I take trips that allows me to sit next to the late Caesar, make eye contact with both siblings, brother and sister, reminding me of Alexander. I am the great! I march into these beats of humanity's feet. Listen closely; you will hear my echoes—not with my being, but with me!

All this space, the enemy we breathe, all of these deceptions, the hope we hold dear—diminish in fear! I will bring you back before god, and you will learn how to love again, love and stare onto us again!

I embrace you, wishing and hoping; they can hear my teardrops as I sleep because every night I weep. I slumber no more. This has lasted for weeks and weeks. I see you beyond these leathers; these are the labyrinths of my letters.

Men of Monsters and Demons

Monsters of men, we demons live within. We win outwardly. Words of secrets. Conversations of time written in tablets.

We spoke through bibles of old. Tablets are broken. Let the feast begin. We're all thankful for your end.

Nobility

You must have an infrastructure of trust, nobility, and faith! For without these you have nothing...

How I Feel

B end, buried down with the hammer of emotions created by your wrath, but lay me to rest where my mother rest. Bare to breath this dust, this debris fluttering in my lungs as I exhale with my sure determination.

I live forcefully! This is how I feel: the aroma of chemistry has me reminiscing about the things that hover between you and I, that caused me a bond that I cannot deny—you see! You're like chapters in my life, fluttering back and forth.

Pin point pages to halt on was never mine to decide. I handed over to the beast that I created in the bed where I lay. This was of God's doing, and what I mean by this is me and you being one in the ocean of unblinding love.

But you see, these chapters were ripped; the story is not as it was told! It wasn't how I imagined it, not toe for toe nor tongue to tongue, tell death do we part. I will deceive—ripped and pulled and tugged on—until it bursts!

These chapters have rigid pages, torn pages where you can't see the marks of its counterpart. A lingering of what was there. A reminder of what was kept. Understand these pages kept our secrets, kept our moments, kept our beginnings. They were never meant to be ripped and turn into ash, to dust, before me.

Allow me to reflect of the gifts you provided me, the present that I can't give back. How do I feel? Is something you can't take back—how I feel? Is unconditional remorse, unconditional compassion, you see, how I feel is how I adore you, the way I would hold you. How I feel is fearful as I could lose you.

But I'm suicidal, content to die without you; to live without you is one of the same! For you have killed me multiple times; you have erased me multiple times only to withdraw me never the same, but you want me to remain to sing these lullaby of lies, but can't you see that even my good-byes aren't even the same...

I can't sing those, not like I once knew how! You took the spark out of my life and replaced it with grief. You see, my love took it and twisted into a beautiful reef that protected me from your tidal wave of clashing emotions. Even then I shiver. I crumble like glass!

How do I feel? I feel like drenched pages, watered-down pages, soaked-in-the-leaves pages—this is how I feel. I feel transparent between my stories. You would like to remain. The end is yours; the beginning is mine.

For what I wish for was never at hand to reach for. How do I feel? I feel like chapters without pages; the book that was created only had ripped pages, markings of my former self! Nonetheless, you would like to write stories on top of stories that you can't take back.

How do I feel? I feel like a book without a hardcover back. I feel like the story without chapters. How do I feel? I feel like I never had an end or beginning, because I realize this book is being created as I speak it. You can call my book the book of possibilities.

How I feel is the probabilities within the possibilities of us! And now it's beyond my comprehension or touch, but I can say sorry—sorry for what you've done, sorry for what I have become. Yet I will become more then you achieved, for what I look for is not retribution; what I look for is complete admiration, for what I have handed over to you, for what I have given you, was taken from a portion of my heart and soul. How I feel I can't describe because you have taken it all.

Good Day

S tanding there with a mystic wonder about you, about your features, about your movements like a cloak of sexuality. I walk to you, providing you with my personality.

So what is your name?

Your reply, "My name is Yesterday," and I reply, "My name is Today. Why don't you and I journey on a date?" You smiled. I smirked. And we created tomorrow.

Secret lies

Neither can you have one without the other: secrets tend to lay in fields of greed and green pipe poppers. See it mimic with repetition of woodpeckers pecking! Secrets hold the keys to the lies, and lies hold the keys to secrets...

If you want to find the truth, you must lie as if you were the truth, lie until you found your secrets, because all secrets lie in between lies. Do be mindful of who you cast this illusion upon, for you cast a beautiful lie on the receiver.

Be aware, for at that very moment you too have cast a lie on one's own self. For the receiver on which you've cast the spell of illusion will carry on as if the illusion is their very own reality, living a lie.

Protecting your secrets is truly harboring a demon and turning you into a puppet while it transforms itself into your puppeteer, slowly consuming your soul, and turns what ifs and maybes into whys, into guilt.

Listen to the words of the wise. We speak tales of old; still it roots deep into layers that bloom containers of chessboards-creating secrets. We use our tongues of lies to form our prison of secrets, these demons that live and dwell within.

These parasites that control our every movement in life; they took hold of us since young, baited us with fear, lured us in with insecurity, and devoured us with a temporary protection, with the small price of our soul. We give over ourselves, so at the end we can lay into the secret of lies.

Bigs

Obesity, you feast as a beast! Bestiality without any reality. Bring senses to the masses—kernel, caption—I can begin to ask you what type of caption. I read the understanding of your flesh, but the corporation is taking the masses for ransom.

Give them cash for more. Aren't they handsome? Increase the ransom; give them more. The cavalry of calories is intact, fabricate, false, experimental products. Inflamed body, colon—disease! Respiratory…tell me why I couldn't breathe? This is the end of the journey.

American…America! The land of the brave, the land of the corporations, and the land of the experimentations. Allow this to be the spring! Do stop taking that out your mind. Do stop taking that out of your mind like I'm speaking about roles, like I'm speaking about spring rolls.

All fabrication, inorganic, enzymes empty, taken into your mind—and what do you have? I can assure is nothing like the allure of the magazine! I lie down onto a bed of fabrication, an on organic product.

Lie with my popcorn, lie with my Snickers, and lie on the bed of the products of my destruction, of my own demise, but who cares? I lie in the bed of America. America, the land of the feed, the land obese beast!

The land of the misery. We live in disillusions because it's for our history. I am pale; I am without pigmentation. What can I say? This is my nation! America, the home of the abomination. We are the plague of the nations.

Blank Story

Blank slate, I am. I'm a blank slate, which I am. My features, I have none! My future is without a face; I have none! My structure is clean, black and white, pearly white! I am pure; I am clean; I am untainted. Why do you try to cling to me?

You hover over me. My shadow doesn't have a shadow. Why are you trying to blend with me, become me? You entangle your tentacles of actions, words all over me! Squeezing and imprinting: love, care, forever, honor…

Used, abused, destroyed! You start redesigning your fears and insecurities of your hopes and dreams all over me. With every stroke, with every carving, you shed blood emotions, forming tears of oceans that flood my mother's moments and submerge my entire being.

Against my will! I do not want to be like you! Stop prying your tentacles up and down my pure slate of a heart. My god-given heartbeat of talents must resist this! I am pure. Why are you carving your name on me, your broken goods on me? Why are you writing your story of past experiences on me?

Why write lies on me? Why write betrayals on me? Why write broken hearts on me? Why write stories on top of my back that amount to twenty-foot stories? They're higher than the tallest skies, because they're full of uneventful moments!

Rip apart. Let my blank life be mine, and live yours. Why write your story on the structure of my futures? My cheeks, my lips—why form them? It's my life, my canvas of essence! Let me—no—allow me to describe it all.

Give me back my canvas! Give me back my flesh! Give me back my will! Give me back my life, and allow me to reflect! I was pure. I was unbroken. I was unmarked. I was untarnished. I have completely erased you, for I have never lost me. I am stain-free, along with this blanket that warms me. It is my story!

Forsake

Let's imagine a night that we want remember, but you and I will live forever. Let's create and describe memories together and throw them into the pile of eternity. Therefore, let our moments now piece the puzzle of our difficulties and our triumphs!

Piece by piece, mistake by mistake, hunger by hunger, we will conquer. Then conquer this place! This moment! We are engraved beyond the grave, anointed and celestially divine by the home of the heavens so that our gaze can last.

Casting the awareness to this beautiful generation, for it was carved by our decisions. This is our image of a legacy, our plateau lying plainly as we, you, shape our sculpture, our table, our reward.

A ladder as tall as…However, when we and whatever scrapes the tip of what we uphold dearest…I've given you all that was at stake. These are the hopes of all you forsook.

Birth

Birth in the tree of star. Lie in the bed of novae; witness my marvels! Travel light years to exit out of my mothers, whom my beloved!

Born as a pharaoh, reforming the blankets of the heavens. I enter the Garden of she, sipping the ocean of their feet and sleeping with the sounds of their hearts. I formed Noah's Ark.

Creating a reality of an imperfect utopia: hers of his, his of hers. Witness the lies of hurt! Let the drought come! The answer is in the why. Live in the destruction of realities while decorating our own moralities.

Sometimes and at times, we drift between our thoughts and become lost souls of our former selves. Take notice: silence will come, peace will take hold, and you will be found again. Souls of moments, creating here and now. You stand to find yourself once again.

Will You

The sun will set its marvelous blaze of glory onto the heavens, and the blankets of this world will be immersed in the light of creation. The clouds will glow, brimming golden ember red, forming east to south, leaving the path to life into your eyes and the keys into everything you feel.

Man of Sea

You know I've been carrying you for a very long while now, and never have I complained! I mean my back is wide, and I have to say that sometimes I lack stability, but that only means that I have more of a meaning to me!

Stand still, and I promise you under any circumstance, I will carry you through! You see, I'm a part of everything, and everything is a part of me. I cling to these lands, and in my belly, I carry wonders.

Creatures you have never seen, but I promise you that I will never swallow you. Never will I take you from these clusters, mists of chemistries, this world! This moment, I need you to breathe these oceans of emotions.

Take in my essence. Let the vapors of my soul give you courage and nourishment so you can know we're still breathing within the cocoon of our love. All the circumstances, probabilities, and chances that we will take together…

May have you create doubts, but set them aside, because I am your captain, and all of this is my outside. Be brave! Because I am brave for you. Love of emotions' seas, I see you! I will shelter you to the land of our seeds. Thank you for your complete company; farewell my enchanted sea queen.

Money Magic

I believe and perceive that we as a collective should call money magic! I mean, you would think that money is the root of all evil, and magic is creating something or making something happen unexplainably just by thinking about it or wanting it.

Magic! A mythical element that some would consider a taboo, yet the concept remains infinite. So how does this actually relate to money? Well, money has the tendency of making you, the individual, do things that under any other circumstances you would not want, nor think to do.

It is as if it urges you to do things unexplainably. It makes things happen without any explanations. So why bother calling it money? Why not just call it magic, since for most of humanity it is the entity that has brought joy.

It is the entity of a key that unlocks their smiles at the end of the day, giving them reasoning to do the things and say the things they say onto each other, you and I, but why not call it magic? Since magic is the root of all evil—even back in the 1600s, medieval times.

Witches and warlocks were shunned. Nonetheless in modern day time—here and now!—the rich are shun and the poor needs more. What are we, as humanity, willing to do? In order to bring forth such remarkable magic—unexplainable happenings!

Well, I will tell you the answer, and it does not have anything to do with magic: it has to do with me and you! Let's help one another, like really! Just help one another freely. It is only once this chasm is filled with our own sincerity of love for one another that we can obtain true joy that won't bind us to anything tangible my dear.

Uniqueness

I am so profound that life found me indifferently unique. Thus, the world's morality gaze failed inevitably on me, with the kiss of immortality, leaving death's maiden to divorce and remarry me. I alone tied the world, along with life and death, into humanity's indifferences. I am profound. You have discovered me!

Inevitably, you will never believe that I got bullied.

Love You

Heart and time were best friends. I remember moments where heart would fall for not going along with the galactic beats of the orchestra symphony, and without a doubt, time was always there to lend a helping hand.

Yet you don't understand. At the end of the school yard were bullies of lies, love, hate, greed, and betrayal. Together they bruised and scarred the rhythm of life out of heart until it resembled an out-of-tune, deformed instrument.

I've always told my heart to not ever fear, for time will always be near! To my heart's astonishment, time was there. For every attempt and every threat, time helped my heart conquer again and again.

Although at moments my heart would feel used—for patience always accompanied time—but time would always be there to patch my heart up. As patience sang life's lullaby back into me, time always would hand my heart a bandage and apply it to my heart's scars.

I will never forget those desert walks, where heat and frustration angelically removed the layers of my beating heart until it was bloody white with a hint of tainted ember, burgundy orange-red...

Time was always near to cast a shade of comfort. Now that I have met you, my heart, I would like to tell you of my confession: "I have always loved you, and I'm sorry at moments I wasn't there like time was, but if I can make it up to you in any way, let this moment be the testimonial statement to that overwhelming want, that whim!"

"I want to take you back within me so that you can beat life's rhythm through me, soul! And if it's okay with you, can I have time and patience accompany you so they can reside within we, inside of me."

My heart was so joyful that I thought of its best friend, eternity. In return, it began to speak to me in rhythms, "Of course I will return to you and will have time and patience along with me, for they have made me whole again."

I was blessed by my heart with a joy that fulfilled my entire life. It wasn't long until time grew into forever, causing me and my heart to beat eternity together, because that's how I learned how to love you.

Control Freely

Perception is quite related to inception, for your perception of me is my inception ability to implant an idea into you, causing you to create a reality that benefits me, we!

Prophecy

I would have shed my flesh and given it to you in order for you to have handed it over to her in our native tongue.

Let space take its place within this flesh so that I can mold my shape-shifter's mobility into my abilities.

In order for me to enter back into this world and reshape your meaning of love, your heart, and rebuild it into the model of god, I have shed my flesh so that my sprit can reclaim and recreate the universe in my hands.

So that it can resemble my flesh, as I shed the love that protects it in order to embody life itself and give you a child that was predestined by your god to you! A gift to we, a seed that cannot be replanted.

Don't ever weep. Take pride and take hold, for what has been weaved and mended together with the strings of destiny is not mortal, and I cannot destroy it.

So that I can anoint every age, every year until we're wise and gray—I was the perfect match of you, and it wasn't because it was destined but because I reshaped myself after you. Thank you!

The Adventurer

How can an adventurer be a failure? For the simple act of adventuring evokes the act of conquest, for adventuring has no end, thus banishing the act of failure, for an adventurer who has never ventured at all has truly evoked the act of failure.

Power of Words

I have the power to break and demolish you. I have the power and the ability to build and destroy you! Understand, you seek me. I took everything about you and ripped it into fragments of its natural state.

Piece them together to create an archer's bow, because I respect you! This is the tradition and condition of my culture: it forms the reconstruction of humanity. Seek me, for my words have the abilities to create fear, dreams, and night terrors.

To break down gates and enter pools where I drown myself into an ocean of lakes and rivers, shifting waves revealing heaven's name. Every door that I conquer, I create the key, a reconstruction combination! I fit it specifically for you, for me, and the selected few—we!

I speak of humanity, for we are beast! Physically and mentally, I reform, because the power of my words has the substance to create strength, stability, and grace. Triumph after triumph. I've gained luxury with my deliverance to change things of your hell, of your dreams drastically!

I am that poet. I am that beginning. I am that architect of artistic art, and my words are your resident, living at the precipice of your perception. Suitably it fancied me; it must be addressed with precise directions. After all, it hast captured my deepest desires perfectly!

My words can bury your heart and suffocate your voice into a muted, macroscopic casket! My word can cause your emotions to vibrate to such a state that we, I, and not even God can see them!

I have the mobility along with the abilities to have my words travel galaxies within celestial dynasty, leaving a fragment of myself behind with each universe my influence descends upon, so every generation of your kind can bring me back into the flow of life.

My words have the power to evoke immortality and cast it on me! I have nothing to say as I drink this cup of ambrosia, marking my existence with every sip. With this tongue I've strived. For well after I'm gone, the power of these words will linger and remain in the soul of humanity well after my leave.

Everything

So it falls and dwindles into magnificent sparkles of the moon. Let the clouds, as I see, do as they please, melting so carelessly and mercifully into the spaceless void. It glows, our rare and radiant anomaly, resembling me, unites in bursts.

Formidably, you put my cup of tea down as its vapors dance into the morning haze, reforming and resembling the Cheshire king. I wonder: will you take a cup of tea with me? And let me then resemble the deceased within we.

I remember when I met you on the shoreline near the sand, mounted on a cliff so elegantly beautiful, head bowed, beautiful breasts complimenting your blouse, mermaid of the sea. You sleep with me, for this immortality night, you became my goddess, a weapon of love and mass destruction. I am your will.

As I breezed along with you, it was worth it! Tight-string walks on destinies, preconceived dreams of our tomorrow as if it were now! This lies in between your elegant jester of a character. I liked the way she licked her.

She resemble her and mimic her, all the positions! I was night, and she was day. She was the moon, and I was the sun. I was her shadow, and she was my flesh; we molded back and forth, creating the shape of our sexuality!

We'll be great buds because we breeze better when we're together—sexy-sativa! I like that gaze. Night marks the constellation of souls, resembling the fierce mythical lion beast that I am.

These are the constellations of what I have become; these are the constellations to us souls. Brave humanity, I bow to no truth, yet as a friend, we understand your disguise. I am brave. Now breeze with me until we collide under the many frequency of life, creating a galactic rainbow of chemistry.

Gliding with my magic carpet over the sea...Perception is everything, and your everything has become our prism, the reflection of our galaxy, and the form of Siamese balance beams. Give me your nightmares, and I'll give you my dreams.

Conquer Power

I have power inside of me! I have so much power inside of me! To where I can do anything. I can feel it coursing through my entire vessel. I am this power! I can feel myself inside this flesh—even on the tips of my fingernails—and I can feel it all over me! Me, over flesh, me…

To have this ability to destroy things of such a fragile nature and yet to resist it; it's almost as if you were playing with a gentle breeze. The key is to be this powerful yet to not destroy something so fragile, something so delicate.

To resist such irresistible urges is to gain a completely different shifting paradigm of an untamed force, for this is when you gain power over your power. You have ascended to the level of the beast, the level of the demons, the level of the demonic, the level of the angels, and the level of the gods.

You have become true state. If you apply this awareness in all areas of your living existence, you will then reap the plentiful bounty of your conquers. For you have claimed your one true state! You, the conqueror of the ego!

Of Us

Mark me with the label of, "Drink me!" I'm bottle tight. Pour all your emotions into me, and I, in return, shall let you drink from me. Carry this label—the one you're holding onto—on your walk, and play your fine tones.

This piano's soothing melodies have beautifully penetrated these ripples of my vibrations. I beg you, let I who you call essence, soul, rise out of your world so that I can rewrite the universe as you and I capture its moments.

This is not family, nor is it familiar. I'm not friendly nor have I ever been needy, but I thank you for feeding me. Woman, you remind me of when we were young and you were beautiful. I loved your pastries. Your pearls always carried this esoteric aroma of plums and saliva, only known by us!

Your nectar. I will have you completely natural before me, so I can sip the world, along with its attachments, out of you slowly. Allow me to fall back and play the thighs of your accordion accordantly to the melodies of your heart's desire.

Bottles full of breeze. I can't believe what I'm watching is dripping and drooping off my sleeves, forming the hour hand. Burgundy drapes, she's beautiful! Tree marks, bear marks, there's a spider, Mrs. Cat Shire...

Please dear, do drink from the ember green dreams. Why you ask? Because it is of us, and we are of the collective collided effect of such romantic chemistry. Be a dear and hand me the answers to our mysteries, and come join me under this tapestry of stars.

Living Beauty

A women's body is born angelically enchanted in every way, in every sector. In every angle and within every curve, their bodies are meant to hypnotize, to put you in a state of hypnosis, rendering their grace complete control over your subconscious.

Her body is a walking perfection of what witches create and cast as beauty. In the halls of the cathedral, she's royally refined, and I have to say that she have captured and bound me!

Pour me into the image of your celestial beauty so I can reflect your personality. I am completely, obsessively in love with everything that was given to you!

Genetically, mentally, and by life itself thoroughly! Hopefully you will be merged with me into this ruby of a gem, into this diamond, this electrical vibration.

You have me excited, selectively destined! I love you. I am a part of you. All of creation has designed you perfectly, uniquely, and precisely for me. You were created with the particle of god's dreams for me, and I was your angel as you slept!

Wake in You

Sincerely befriend you, seriously not offend you. May I have a seat before you? Have lunch with me! I will request, and I will caress every thought that forms the wrinkles of your mind.

You will have me. Remember that we might meet by the week's end of December to enjoy brunch, for by the end of the day I will have you for lunch!

I will turn this misty evening into a remarkable film that you will call glory—trust me! Let your wish turn my generosity into a gem that resembles you and me. I claim and proclaim that tomorrow is ours.

Like the stars we dance with the reflection of eternity in our eyes while our feet move like sparks and flames to our moves. Will you allow me to take this moment to acknowledge every probability that collided to create our union?

Here we lay in currents of tomorrow and today where only the merger of the two—is it real?—obtained it and gained this. I had you before you ended and we said good-bye.

Manifesting Love

We all hold the mystical ability to fall in love with ourselves and or within another, always assuming we have found ourselves—that one! That warm place in between space and moments that vibrates and caresses the surface of your flesh with the slightest gestures. The spectacular conversion of the union sends ripples of inner emotions, manifesting the blooming of love—our ritual of flesh to flesh of that love.

We all have tasted that or some type of indescribable love, but how do we love back? How do we truly love back beyond the perception of our meaning of love? I mean being heartbroken, being let down, being betrayed.

Is that all beneath layers of our own desires being projected onto another? Is that not a form of entrapment? That we lovers cast upon one another so willingly, so freely that we encage each other into a cage of claims.

Of ungrowth possibility: I mean, love, if I'm not mistaken, should promote growth! But why does love—the love we fall in love with—claim one another solely to each other?

Forming the realization that suppresses the boundaries of our true being into a mental void of limbo of an egoistic state to where we no longer grow as individuals or as one singularity, for the moment we fall in love with that one, that anomaly!

We inquire the question of: why can't love also transcend? To appoint where love promotes, supports, and molds you into a better you! To where every soul on the face of this physical plain that our kind calls earth nurtures others with the true essence of unbiased, unconditional love...

To where the light in us increases equally to a point that we no longer have a shade to dim to balance is claimed. Why can't we enter a new we, a new awareness? I believe that love is an undeniable element of truth, which, if looked upon with the gaze of complete freedom, you will notice that I have loved you!

It's like the air that we breathe. I need you to inhale me so that when you exhale me, I can so freely love the world. You see, I'm like that air that you love and that you need, because I help you live as you give meaning to my existence.

To one another, merge together—we grow together! Allow me to be your oxygen so that you can come to know my flavors of life. But I can no longer remain in your lungs cradling your heart; I have fallen in love with the souls of humanity.

I'm in a place that creates similarities that will awaken one reality, and it's that we are love, loving one another. So allow me to say thank you and that I love you for allowing me to be a better me—each and every one of you!

Red Umbrella

Everyday life streams from my eyes. Twenty-nine never knew what thirty learned, and tomorrow can't wait to reveal what you will become! Yet it matters not what form it may take; weather the storm. For it will bleed on you, drip by drip, until that umbrella, that invisible umbrella that coats your very body, your very being, turns bloodshot red.

Let it parcel you from the heavens! Let it always mark your existence, that your inheritance will become your greatest feats and conquest. That this world and knowing what you are inside of it is but a seed waiting to sprout and bloom out the earth of your bed!

Can you prepare yourself for the season to come?

Can you move out the way and let you become the greatness that you are? Ascension is inevitable!

Did I mention that you are celestial being? Did I mention that you were selected and chosen to be manifested onto this reality?

These are not my dreams. These are the realities that we kept from we! Hearing the sounds echo back the words, I did not hear us scream.

That inside of you and knowing what you are, doesn't it rattle whenever it is cold, whenever it is hot, whenever you heed these words and then when you begin to hear these words?

I will hear these words move inside your flesh and know that you're more! One by one, absorb these words.

For this umbrella has been my bloodshot bouquet of roses.

Do you see the road I've chosen so that you can awaken?

Thank you; this is your show.

Money

I'm the greatest illusion that has ever been created by man—by that se-lected few, those powers, the ones that are awakened—that's aware yet abuses the knowing of self!

I cast a net of hysteria so sublime, so uniquely refined, so mixed with I that it blinded the rest of humanity into the ground of mud, despair, and grief until it breached the boarders of their psyche without any relief.

Listen, I travel! To Europe, Spain, Africa, Japan, England, America, North America, and South America. I mean my greed engulfed even beneath the Golf Coast Pacific Ocean! East, West, whatever waste you can come up with...

I am the monarch of the corruption that leaves its mark! I am multi-dimensional colors. I am green. I am nickel. I am dime. I am the trees you cut down and grind.

I am everything beneath the ground that you dig and search through for diamonds and gold, ransom and hopes, only to replenish it all into me. I am valuable! I am that illusion that was design by man, those few selected empowered, infused, awakened souls.

Those individuals control the masses of humanity with such a grip. Truly I can purchase your soul. I can purchase your pride. I can purchase your dignity. I can take everything you stand for and take it into a loop of defeat.

I am the greatest illusion that those elite individuals have ever created. I am known as what you call Money; deposit me! They let you use me so that I can bribe you along with all your relations—your brothers, your sisters—allowing me to create anger and mayhem, so you can release them out of their bodies.

I am that illusion. Please, let me pile bodies on top of bodies without any sight of you. Because I will take the egoistical state of yours and place it in the forefront of your frontal lobe and let your soul drown while I empower the egoist with a crown that tramples all over your immortal substance of life.

Turning you into an unfamiliar entity, I am that greater illusion that has captured the rest of you humans into a mental entrapment of my own illusions. But do believe that whatever is mine is not yours; it's yours! Thank you for allowing me to bribe and dine with you. You're my bride, a bitch of a bribe; I am that bitch! Please rewind.

Remember We

Every day we take an unconscious decision to gamble everything. We're not even aware of it, going on with our daily lives, conditioned. From the moment we're born to the moment we enter elementary and exit their universities…

We were being refined for their workforce formula: a mass production of mental slave to be dispersed into cubicles and factories, where you and I, my friend, are simply part of the equation.

Being plugged in for a particular desired outcome, which profits an un-ending income, and a majority of it all doesn't favor us, as it favors the ones who deploy such a formula!

Stacking one after the other to create an outcome in order to enslave the next generations to come. Who among us has the strength to awaken from such a spell, such an entrenched entrapment of an illusion, in order to gain stability mentally?

Stable your thoughts, control them. Remember we need to keep near to the awareness that we are soul. We must take heed of this, for if not, our egotistic mind will run freely, and we will be the esoteric beings on which it gallops so proudly as it confirms its quest of domination.

I wish for all the souls on this label "earth" to, for one moment, take captive of their awareness and rise to the surface of their conditions and claim what is rightfully theirs. For we are consciousness that will take back our natural state from the egoistic instrument of our minds.

At moments it would take a near death experience or some type of trauma to drop the veil of illusion, and for that second, for that moment, we were we again, soul—completely aware of our astronomically infinite state of being pure energy, correlating infinitely inside the body of creation.

Don't let it slip, because I did not! I captured and reawakened myself. Yes, I could've stayed in the matrix. I could've stayed in the illusion and remained hidden in their formula forever, and who knows? I could have reaped all of the benefits from their formula, because what I am aware of allows me to manipulate their calculations to befit me.

I could've been further with a lot more riches, power, and material objects—all of it! I chose otherwise: the knowing that I could have obtained every worldly possession that my heart ever craved, but at the end it means nothing if I don't have myself! If I can't express myself, then what am I expressing? Is it the preconceived notion of society's perception of what should be or should not be?

Then we at the end are contently just living a miserable, preconditioned existence that erases you, soul entirely. You become nothing more but a drone waiting to encounter your exit end, yet I ask you, have these words awakened you and stabilized your hopes a little? Have they ignited flames in your psyche? I hope all societies and all of humanity feels the tremors of these words within the walls of their realities.

My Speaking Tongue

Something needs to be done, something further! I need to twist this tongue into a shape that can't be mimicked; something needs to be done! Something more...

Something with me—you don't understand. I need to twist this tongue into a form that can't be mimicked, that cannot be ripped out and duplicated, that cannot be undone.

I need to throw myself into the world and let myself, I, soul, absorb every bit of her fading fragments so that I can regurgitate its majestic elements into an art form that all the worlds would embrace...

Like a new breed of lilies that have sketched their evolution on existence manifestations of life, entering a reality vastly consumed with my resonance, a clarity pressure so refined that it allowed you! Soul to deeply slumber for nevermore; this is the spell of my allure.

I need to create a scent that transforms me, soul, into an aroma that resonates my existence throughout the worlds. Let not mortality disguise its misdirection of my mortal heart.

I am that ability. I seek it entirely. I am poetry! I am the gift that will change the destruction in humanity's armor of ill moralities. I will bring them all into my reality with this deformed, retwisted, encrypted tongue.

My speaking word, word speaking, keep these words. The truth is in our art for everlasting. It's the spell of our crafting, it will not be banned!

Made in the USA
Columbia, SC
19 January 2019